Sample page with animal and monster designs for metal engravers,
by Master E.S., Upper Rhenish, 1440-1467

BIG BOOK OF
DRAGONS, MONSTERS,
AND OTHER MYTHICAL CREATURES

Ernst and Johanna Lehner

DOVER PUBLICATIONS, INC.
Mineola, New York

Bibliographical Note

This Dover edition, first published in 2004, is an unabridged republication of *A Fantastic Bestiary: Beasts and Monsters in Myth and Folklore*, originally published by Tudor Publishing Company, New York, in 1969.

DOVER *Pictorial Archive* SERIES

International Standard Book Number: 0-486-43512-1

Manufactured in the United States of America
Dover Publications, Inc., 31 East 2nd Street, Mineola, N.Y. 11501

CONTENTS

Chapter 8

Chapter 9

Chapter 10

Chapter 11

FOREWORD

Artistic freedom is a fairly modern innovation. The artists of antiquity and the Middle Ages, indeed those of the Renaissance, were bound by dictated conventions of imagery and style. They were artists nonetheless, and, despite these obstacles, found suitable avenues for the expression of fancy, wit and imagination. One such area, which seems perennially to have fascinated them, was the creation of imaginary animals, based on superstition, legend, myth, or simply the free play of their own invention.

The Greek and Roman artist drew from the rich storehouse of classic myth to represent such creatures as the Gorgon, the Harpy, the Sphinx, the Pegasus. In Islamic times, the Musulman craftsman, prevented by Mahomet's strictures from making natural representations, skirted Koranic law, and risked eternal damnation, by turning to the unnatural — weaving into his designs strange forms that were part human, part animal, part vegetable. His counterpart in Medieval Europe, acting on similar impulses, worked the image of Gargonille, the popular folk legend dragon, into the decorations of the church of the Ile de France.

Scriptures, received texts, epics provided the artist with a staggering array of demons, monsters and anthropomorphic terrors. The Chinese tale of the battle of Gautama with the bizarre monster army of Mara was translated nearly image for image on the walls of the Caves of the Thousand Buddhas at Tunhuang (T'ang Dynasty). In the West, the Temptations of St. Anthony and the dismal eschatological passages from the Apocalypse (Book of Revelations), with their numerous monsters and unearthly creatures, became standard themes for artistic composition.

There were still other sources. Assembled in the tenth century and much read in the Middle Ages was the *Picatrix*, literally a treatise on magic practices employing astrology. The formulas for magical control called for the making of likenesses of gods and demons and fifty are described for the use of the simulator—a pitifully small number when compared to the 16th-century demonographer Feyerabend, who in his *Theatrum Diabolum* lists over two-and-a-half trillion devils. For the more scholarly artist there was much to be learned from Boccaccio's *Genealogia Deorum*, a compendium of mythological gods and beasts. Adding to the fabulous terrors that abounded were the grossly distorted, yet highly imaginative tales of travelers. Schedel's *Chronicle of the World,* published in Nürnberg in 1498, cites, as a few of the witnessed marvels of the East, cynophali or dog-faced, barking men and sciopedes, humans with but one leg ending in a monstrous foot. The Unicorn itself, of Indian ancestry, came to Europe via Pliny's *Natural History* and is undoubtedly a somewhat inaccurate account of the rhinoceros.

Since the close of the Middle Ages, any number of artists have heeded the pronouncement of Dürer that, "If a person wants to create the stuff that dreams are made of, let him freely mix all sorts of creatures." During the Renaissance, such strange forms were designated "grotteschi," whence our word "grotesque," referring to an ornamental style suggested by some relics from antiquity found in a grotto-like structure in Rome—sinister, playful and unfamiliar. Bosch and Breughel are the most well-known members of this stylistic company, but it is well to remember that Raphael made ornamental grotesques for the pillars of the papal loggias. Leonardo da Vinci, Signorelli, Grünewald and a host of others were also known for their indulgence in monster-making.

Nor did the interest cease with the beginning of modern art and the onset of the age of science: Odilon Redon, James Ensor, John Graham and, more recently, Robert Beauchamp are among the artists who have continued the fascination for demonic and fantastic form. The curious manifestations of dreams and of the subliminal mental life, with all their attendant oddities of substance and contradictory juxtapositions, are still of singular concern to artists. The Surrealist and Dada movements deliberately attempted to investigate such phenomena, and elements of contemporary Pop and Funk art still bear witness to that search. Dürer's observation is echoed in our time by Joseph Campbell's:

The unconscious sends all sorts of vapors, odd beings, terrors and deluding images up into the mind — whether in dream, broad daylight, or insanity; for the human kingdom beneath the floor of the comparatively neat little dwelling that we call our consciousness, goes down into unsuspected Aladdin's caves. (*The Hero With a Thousand Faces*)

HENRY P. RALEIGH
Chairman, Division of Art
State University College
New Paltz, New York

INTRODUCTION

Nowhere else has the human fantasy, triggered by fear of the unknown or inexplicable in nature, shown a wider scope than in the invention of fanciful or grotesque monsters. In his imagination, pre-scientific man saw monsters everywhere — on land, in the waters and in the air — embodying all facets of his anxieties. The basic idea of the existence of monsters is actually not so far-fetched as it might appear from our first look at the nasty creatures that haunted the thoughts and fantasies of our forebears. There was a time, in the beginning of human history, when animals, against whose power and cunning man had little defense, were considered gods. Their behavior inspired man to assign to them appropriate powers, names and spirits. Man also feared that the souls of slain animals, unless propitiated, might take

revenge, or that a man's soul after his death would sometimes enter the body of an animal. Animals were thus worshipped before gods were created. Later, they became associated with the newer deities and were mummified after death as their sacred representatives. In the earlier religions we find deities represented with the bodies of men and the heads of animals, or vice versa, or as fabulous, fantastic creatures who combined different parts of different kinds of beasts. The ancient Assyrian-Babylonian and Egyptian mythologies abound with such composite monster-gods. Many theories as to the origin and cause of monsters were advanced in bygone times: in ancient mythologies they were the offspring of the union of humans with gods in animal disguise; a common belief in folklore attributed them

The Biblical monsters *Behemoth* and *Leviathan* (Job 40:15),
designed and printed by William Blake, London, 1825

to the unnatural intercourse of different species of animals; while according to medieval theology such creatures were believed to be the outcome of copulation by infernal creatures with witches. In earliest times and in primitive beliefs, animal sacrifices were related to the deep-seated ancient tendency in man to identify himself with the power and spirit of the slain animal. Prehistoric man coveted the mysterious personality of beasts whose skins, tails, horns and feathers were not only worn as clothing and decoration, but also for their magical virtues. Many of the beasts encountered by man in these times were awe-inspiring in their strength, ferocity, or gruesome appearance, and so man adopted their characteristics for himself. He not only used the adornments of the animals but also used their names and replicas later on in cognomina, titles and heraldic devices; as in the escutcheons of medieval knights; the family totem poles of the Indians of Alaska and British Columbia; the half-human, half-animal family gods of Polynesia; or the religious animal dance

masks of Africa, North and South America and the Far East. All this use of animal and monster images was primarily to endow the user with the heroic features of the beast represented, and to frighten away evil spirits and demons. Looking at the most outstanding characteristics of monsters of bygone days, we find that even today there are animals which show some of these monstrous features: for size we still have the pachyderms: elephant, rhinoceros and hippopotamus; for ferocity, the carnivorous beasts: lion, tiger, wolf and others; for dragon-like ugliness, the reptiles: crocodile, cayman, gavial, alligator, chameleon, iguana, Gila monster and others; for grotesqueness: the dromedary, giraffe, hyena, and gorilla; for deadliness: the boa constrictor, cobra, rattlesnake and other poisonous serpents; for hideous looking insects: the scorpion, blackwidow spider, praying mantis, and molecricket; for sea-monsters: the hammerhead shark, manta-ray, moray, and man-of-war; and for flying monsters: the vampire bat, vulture, condor and other birds of prey.

St. John in Patmos and the seven-headed red dragon (Revelation 12:3), from Phil. Floury's *Compendiosa*, printed by Jean Merausse, Paris, 1510

The Whore of Babylon riding the seven-headed dragon, from *Das Neue Testament*,
designed by Hans Burgkmair, printed by Silvan Othmar, Augsburg, 1523

Strange monsters on land, in the sea and the air, from Conrad von Megenberg's
Puch der Natur, printed by Johann Baemler, Augsburg, 1478

LIST OF ILLUSTRATIONS

St. Michael slaying the dragon of sin (Revelation 12:9), from an Anglo-Saxon manuscript Bible, 11th century

14 ～ ILLUSTRATIONS

**The capture of the unicorn (medieval Christian legend)
from a medieval manuscript Bible, 13th Century**

**Eve and the serpent of sin, from *Speculum humanae salvationis*,
printed by Günther Zainer, Augsburg, 1470**

The dragon-mouth of hell, from *Das Buch Belial*, printed by Jacobus de Teramo, Augsburg, 1473

**The altar of the ox-headed deity, *Moloch*, at Gehinnom (Amos 5:26),
from Athanasius Kircher's *Oedipus Aegyptiacus*, Rome, 1652**

Chapter 1

DRAGONS

The dragon is one of the oldest, most widespread and persistent monsters in occidental mythology, religion and folklore. It is a four-elemental beast: there were subterranean dragons, aquatic dragons, dragons of the air, and fire-breathing dragons. All dragons in Western myths were sinister, terrifying creatures, emblematic of destructive, evil and anarchical principles. The dragon-slaying mythological and religious folk-hero or saint was also strictly a feature of the Western world, from the Euphrates in the east to the Iberian peninsula in the west, and from the Nile valley in the south to the Teutonic forests in the north. In antiquity there was the Greek sun-god Apollo, who slew the dragon-serpent *Python*, guardian of the chasms of darkness on Mount Parnassus; and the legendary Phoenician prince Cadmus who killed a dragon sacred to Mars. From the teeth of this dragon, which he sowed in the earth, armed men sprang up and proceeded to fight each other until only five were left alive. These five helped Cadmus found and build the city of Thebes. In medieval times there were dragon-slaying folk-heroes such as Siegfried, hero of the Teutonic *Nibelungenlied,* who killed the dragon *Fafnir,* guardian of the Nibelungen Hoard; or Beowulf, hero of the Anglo-Saxon epic, who slew the treasure-guarding dragon ravaging his kingdom, Geates. Christian lore is full of saints who have fought, killed or transfixed many an evil dragon: St. George, St. Margaret, St. Martha, St. Romain, St. Samson, St. Philip of Bethsaida and many more. The dragon image was widely used in medieval times in the Western world to symbolize evil — in religious works, in mystic and magic philosophies, in Gnostic and Rosicrucian emblem books, and in demonology, astrology and alchemy, as the representation of the devil, hell, sin, heresy, darkness, superstition, and other evil capacities.

Dragon killing an elephant, from a 12th-century bestiary manuscript

The Wyvern of Merlin, from an enameled sorcerer's amulet,
France, early 15th century

Poliphili and the dragon, from Franciscus Columna's *Hypnerotomachia
Poliphili*, printed by Aldus Manutius, Venice, 1499

Dragon, after Lucas (Hugensz) van Leyden, Holland (1494-1533)

**Mother dragons fighting for their young, from a French
calligraphic manuscript, Paris, 15th century**

The dragon-slayer St. Margereth of Antioch, from Lucas Cranach the
Elder's *Wittemberger Heiligthumbuch*, Wittenberg, 1509

Hercules slaying the dragon *Ladon*, from Othmar Brunfels'
Herbarium, printed by Johannes Schott, Strassburg, 1530

Dragonel, a young dragon, by Pierre Belon, 1553

The dragon-slayer Ruggeretto, from Panfilo di Renaldini's *Innamorata di Ruggeretto,* printed by Comin da Trino do Monferrato, Venice, 1555

Sea dragon, from Boaistuau's *Histoires prodigieuses*, Paris, 1576

Seven-headed dragon, from Conrad Lycosthenes' *Prodigiorum* ac
ostentorum chronicon, printed by Henry Petri, Basle, 1557

The dragon-slayer St. George, from Edmund Spenser's *The Faerie Queene*,
printed by William Ponsonby, London, 1590

Draco Aethiopicus, from Ulysses Aldrovandus' *Serpentum
et Draconium Historiae*, Bologna, 1640

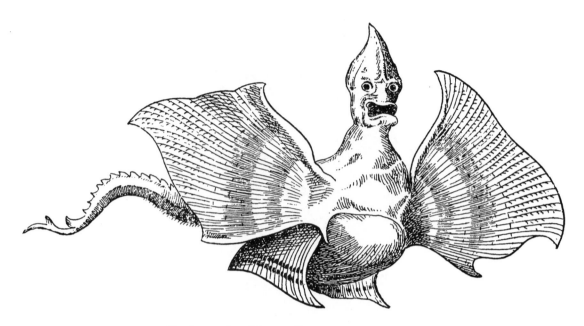

Sky dragon, from Ulysses Aldrovandus' *Serpentum et
Draconium Historiae*, Bologna, 1640

The two-legged dragon-worm of Milan, from Ulysses Aldrovandus'
Serpentum et Draconium Historiae, Bologna, 1640

The demonic horned dragon of Hell, from a pen drawing in an
old French manuscript, *La Magie noire*, Paris, 19th century

The dragon of the deep sea, after Ambrosinus, 1642

The *Lindwurm* was not actually a dragon, but a winged monster serpent, without legs or claws, whose scaly armor glowed in brilliant green-gold or green-silver. In Germanic-Nordic folk-sagas and Middle High German epic poems of knightly love and heroic deeds, it was the guardian of hidden treasures and of beautiful maidens in distress.

The legless, winged *Lindwurm*, a giant dragon-like serpent of Germanic-Nordic folklore and hero-sagas

The *Tatzlwurms* of the Pilatus Mountain, from Athanasius Kircher's *Mundus Subterraneus*

The *Tatzlwurm* was another of the dragon-like monsters of Germanic folklore; a gigantic, winged, fire-breathing serpent with four legs and claws. It dwelled in the crags and caves of the Alpine mountains of Austria, Bavaria and Switzerland, and was the terror of the Alpine peasantry, preying on their cattle and on lost children.

The four-footed, winged *Tatzlwurm*, a dragon-like giant
serpent of Alpine Germanic folklore

The *Tatzlwurm* of *Dracken feldt*, from Athanasius
Kircher's *Mundus Subterraneus*

Symbolic representation of the Dragon of Evil, feeding on and destroying itself,
from a secret Rosicrucian emblem book, 16th century

The *Luminaries* (Light and Knowledge) slaying the Dragons of Evil (Darkness
and Superstition), from a secret Rosicrucian emblem book, 16th century

Hermaphroditus standing over the alchemic Dragon of Chaos,
from H. Jamsthaler's *Viatorium Spagyricum*, Frankfort/M., 1625

The two-headed alchemic dragon, symbolizing the *Materia Prima*, from
Elias Ashmole's *Theatrum Chemicum Britannicum*, London, 1652

The alchemic Sky Dragon, linking the sun and the moon,
from Basil Valentin's *L'Asoth des philosophes*, Paris, 1660

The hermetic dragon-monster, holding the *Massa Confusa* (Chaos) together,
from *Hermaphrodisches Sonn- und Mondskind*, Mainz, 1752

The Dragon of Darkness, from an English chapbook, *A Timely Warning to Rash and Disobedient Children*, Edinburgh, 1721

The dragon *Diabolus*, from John Bunyan's *The Holy War made by Shaddai upon Diabolus*, printed by Dorman Newman and Benjamin Alsop, London, 1682

The alchemic Sky Dragon linking the sun and the moon, from Hans Singriener's
Vögelin Praktik, designed by V. Feil, Vienna, 1534

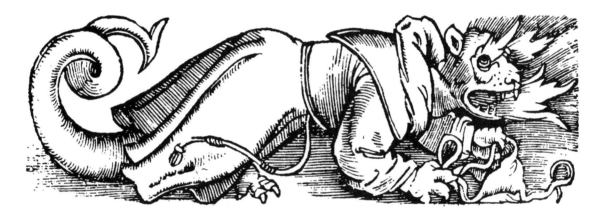

The Dragon of Heresy, from Matthaeus Guidius' *Dialogy*, printed in Switzerland, 1521

The two-headed dragon, symbolizing the calamities at inferior conjunction
of Venus and the sun, from a Mayan stone carving at Copan, Mexico

Two-headed dragon design from a Guetar Indian bowl, San Isidoro

Two-headed *Chimu* dragon design, from a painted Peruvian clay pitcher, Truxillo

Chapter 2

ORIENTAL DRAGONS

Dragons are also important beasts in Far Eastern mythologies, but there is a deeply marked difference in their symbolic meaning: they are not the vicious monsters of the medieval Western world, but friendly, lovable and benevolent creatures. They are the genii of strength, the emblems of vigilance and protection, the guardians of treasures and wisdom. Among the Chinese and the Japanese, dragons are the most potent symbols of the beneficent, rain-giving powers of the gods of water and clouds, and of power, royalty, and sovereignty. In Japan the dragon is the emblem of the Mikado, and in China of the Emperor. China alone has four important groups of protective dragons: the *Tien-Lung*, celestial guardians of the mansions of the gods; the creator dragons of wind, clouds and rain for the benefit of mankind; the *Li-Lung*, benevolent earth, sky and water dragons which ascend to the sky as water-

spouts or typhoons; and the guardian dragons of wealth and wisdom. In Chinese mythology the dragon is one of the four important types of intelligent and protective beasts, the chief of the scaly reptiles. (The other three are the *Unicorn* — king of the hairy beasts; the *Phoenix* — lord of the feathered creatures; and the *Tortoise* — master of the shelled animals.) In Persian mythology the dragon *Azhdaha* is the guardian of all *ganj* — the subterranean treasures of the earth. One of the most important and colorful Oriental festivals is the *Chinese Dragon Boat Festival*, during which dragon-shaped boats are raced on all waterways in China, and special rice cakes dedicated to His Majesty the Dragon are eaten by a merrymaking crowd. This festival is in reality a nation-wide prayer for a good harvest resulting from the fecund rains of which *Lung* — the Dragon — is the celestial guardian.

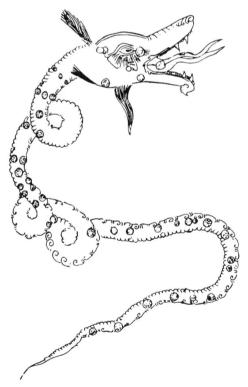

Al-Thu'ban, the constellation Draco, from an ancient Arabic astronomic manuscript

Pi-hsi, the dragon-tortoise god of the rivers, symbol of enormous
strength, from an old Chinese engraving

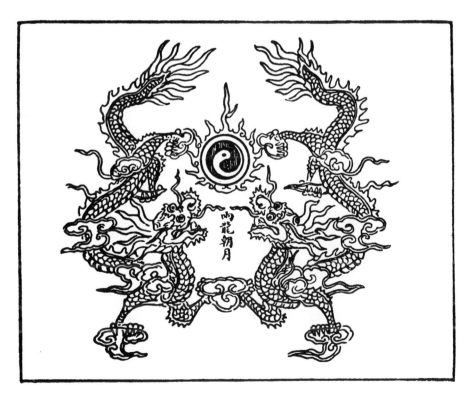

Chen-lung, the guardian dragons, from an old Chinese engraving

Chinese dragon, from an old lantern silhouette

The Dragon of Longevity, from a mural tablet in the Temple of
Longevity, Canton, China

The dragon emblem of the Chinese emperor, symbol of creative power,
from a Chinese lantern silhouette

The Dragons of the Clouds and of the Sea, from an old Chinese engraving

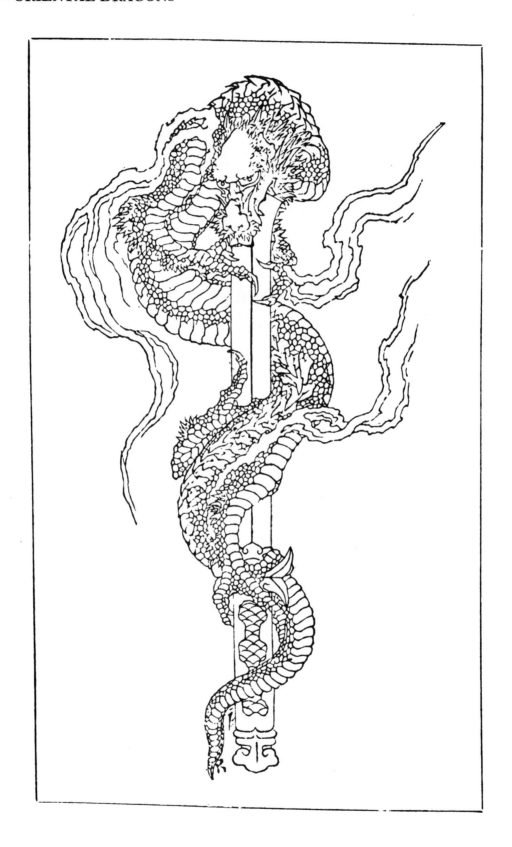

Heaven's cloud-gathering sword, *Murakumo-no-tsurugi*, one of the three Japanese
Imperial treasures, found in the tail of a dragon, designed by Hokusai

The dragon *Ryu,* from an old Japanese pen drawing

The descending and ascending dragons *Ryuto-dabi* (dragon-head and
snake-tail), from an old Japanese engraving

Chapter 3

SERPENT MONSTERS

Since time immemorial, man has feared the serpents. Their subtle and rapid movements, the swiftness of their attack, their venom, their secret hiding places make them the most dangerous and potent monsters in the imagination of mankind. Their ability to shed their skins caused them to be regarded as possessing perpetual youth and everlasting life. They were considered as incomprehensible as destiny, able to conceal themselves even where there were only small stones and short grass. Their ability to live for long periods without food made them seem like mysterious gods. In ancient days there was virtually no religion or philosophy, no native lore or body of legend, no magic or mystic system of belief, that did not assign important functions to serpents. In many mythologies, the monster serpent is not only the beast of chaos and destruction, but also of creation. In the Assyrian-Babylonian religion, Marduc, the creator, slew the serpent monster of chaos, *Tiamat*, splitting it in two and creating from one half the earth, and from the other the sky. The demonic three-headed serpent *Azhi Dahaka*, of ancient Persian mythology, was the symbol of the destructive *and* the generative powers of the earth; the Nordic serpent monster *Nidhoggr*, living in Hel, the primordial abyss, represented the vulcanic powers of the earth; *Cecrops*, the half man, half serpent of Greek mythology, first king of Attica, was the traditional founder of civilization, and of Athens, the citadel of which was called *Cecropia.* In Chinese mythology the woman-headed serpent *Nü-kua-shi* was the world creator. The monster serpent symbol was prominent in the beliefs of the Gnostics, the Rosicrucians, the Ophites and other mystic or Satanist societies, and was used by the astrologers and alchemists. We also find serpent monsters in the myths and lore of almost every tribe in Africa, Asia and America, where they appear mostly in the role of villain, symbolizing everything that is disruptive or evil.

Azon, the ancient Persian god of creative motion, with the serpentine wheel of the Spirit of Life

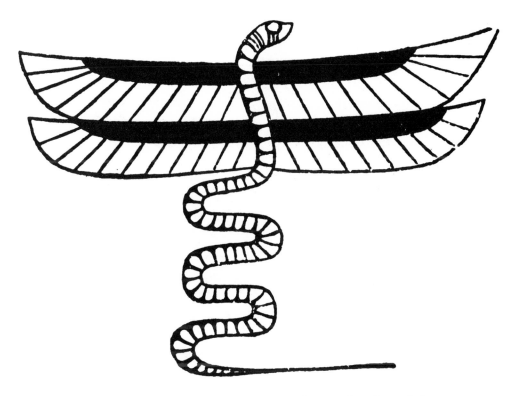

Chanuphis, or *Bait*, the four-winged serpent of ancient Egyptian mythology

Uazit, the tutelary goddess of the ancient Egyptian North,
in the form of a winged uraeus

Cecrops, legendary first king of Attica, half man, half serpent,
from an antique Greek vase painting

The serpents of Poseidon strangling Laocoön and his sons (Greek mythology)

The serpent-footed *Giant*, from an antique Roman wall carving

Heracles and Iolans killing *Hydra*, the many-headed serpent of Lerna,
after an antique Greek vase painting

Abraxas, the serpent-legged god of magical influence, from an
antique Gnostic amulet to ward off witchcraft

The seven-headed Serpent of Fate, from an antique Gnostic seal

Ophiuchus, the Serpent-carrier, worshipped as a constellation by the ancient
Satanist society of Ophites, from an Arabic astronomical manuscript

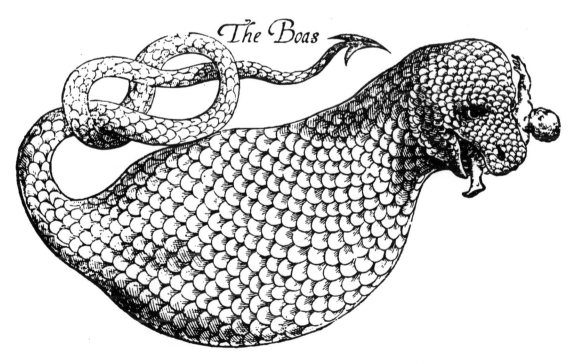

The *Boas,* from Edward Topsell's *A History of Four-Footed Beasts,*
printed at London, 1658

The two-headed Amphisbaena,
from a 12th century bestiary manuscript

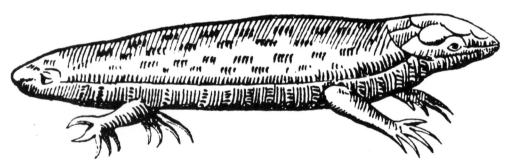

The Amphisbaena as a two-headed lizard, from Aldrovandus'
Serpentum et Draconium Historiae, Bologna, 1640

Multiple-headed serpents, from Münster's *De Africae regionibus*

Symbolic representation of the Serpent of Immorality worshipping before the
Altar of Lust, from a secret Rosicrucian emblem book, 16th century

Entwined serpents, symbol of physical and spiritual union,
from a French emblem, Lyons, 1559

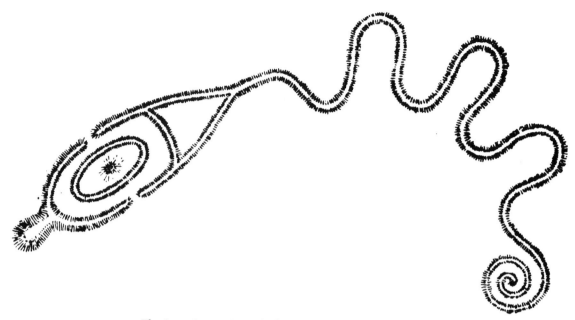

The Great Serpent Mound, about 500 feet long, erected by the
prehistoric mound builders at Adams County, Ohio

Serpent's head, a prehistoric mound builders' copper plate artifact,
from the Hopwell Mound, Ross County, Ohio

Flying serpents, an ornamental design
by the ancient Indians of the Mississippi Valley

Prehistoric shell gorget, a mound builders' rattlesnake charm
from the MacMahan Mound, Sevierville, Tennessee

Feathered serpent, from a prehistoric ceramic plate,
ancient Mississippi Indians

Quetzlal, the plumed serpent bird, symbol of the air,
from an Aztec wall carving, Palenque, Mexico

Kukulcan, the plumed serpent, from a Mayan
wall carving, Yaxchilan, Chiapas, Mexico

Mayan rain serpent, from the
Codex Cortes manuscript

Incan serpent monster, from the
Quechuan Indians

Feathered serpent, a mythological symbol of the
Nicarao Indians, Lake Managua, Nicaragua

Couatl, serpent monster of the Huaxtec Indians,
Veracruz, Mexico

The mythological snake monster
of the Sia Pueblo Indians

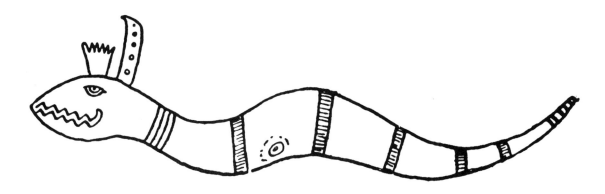

Baho-li-kong-ya, the horned serpent, fertility symbol
of the Moki Indians, Seggy Canyon, Arizona

Avan Yu, the serpent of the underworld,
Pueblo Indians, San Ildefonso, New Mexico

The lightning snake monster,
Nootka Indians, British Columbia

The plumed serpents of lightning, thunder and rain,
from a Tewa Indian pottery decoration, San Ildefonso, New Mexico

Unk-ta-he, the great horned serpent god
of the Algonquin Indians

The mythical serpent *Pal-rai-yuk*,
from an ancient Eskimo bone carving

The woman-headed serpent of creation
(Chinese mythology)

The dragon-headed serpent of the marshes
(Chinese mythology)

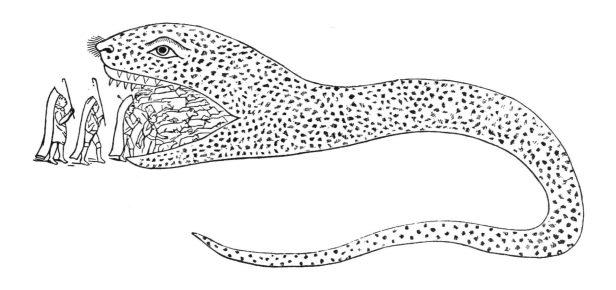

Avatar of Krishna,
from an old Hindu engraving

Sesha, the seven-headed naga-serpent serving as Vishnu's couch and canopy
for the birth of Brahma, from an old Hindu engraving

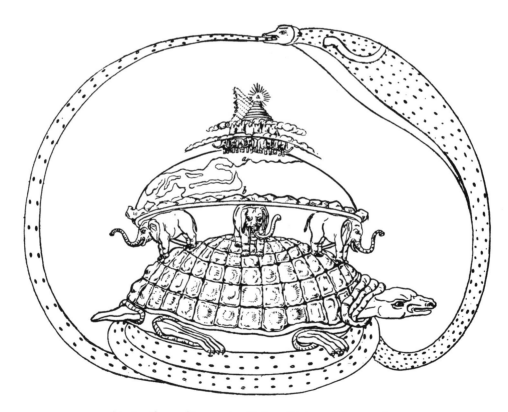

Asootee, the world serpent, with its tail in its mouth, encircling
the three worlds, from an ancient Hindu ceramic

THE OUROBOROS

The serpent biting its own tail, the *Ouroboros,* is an ancient sign of eternity, symbolizing the endless succession of incarnations which form the wheel of eternal life. The Gnostics, an early Christian sect, propagated a system of mystical religious and philosophical doctrines that combined Christianity with Greek and Oriental philosophies. They transformed the evil serpent of Paradise into the beneficent Ouroboros, which they worshipped because it was the serpent who had planted in man's heart the yearning for more knowledge. The medieval alchemists adopted the Gnostic Ouroboros, changing it to the *Hermetic Dragon,* who, in biting its own tail, prevented the transmutation of the elements, and had to be killed before an alchemic experiment could be successfully concluded. In its alchemical representation, the Ouroboros' body is divided into light and dark portions, signifying that good and bad, perfection and inferiority, are bound together in *matter,* like day and night, because alchemical matter is *one* and all-embracing. In ancient astrology the sign of the serpent devouring its own tail was considered the symbolic representation of wisdom. In many ancient beliefs, the tail-biting serpent is the world serpent, like *Midgard* in Teutonic mythology; or *Asootee,* the world-encircling serpent of the Hindu religion, symbolizing the eternal path of the sun.

The oldest extant representation of *Ouroboros,* after the woman alchemist
Cleopatra's *Chrysopeia,* from *Codex Marcianus,* Venice, 11th century

The dragon *Ouroboros*, from an old magic manuscript,
La Magie noire, France

The Basilisk as *Ouroboros*, symbol of the Aeon,
from Horapollo's *Selecta Hierogryphica*, Rome, 1597

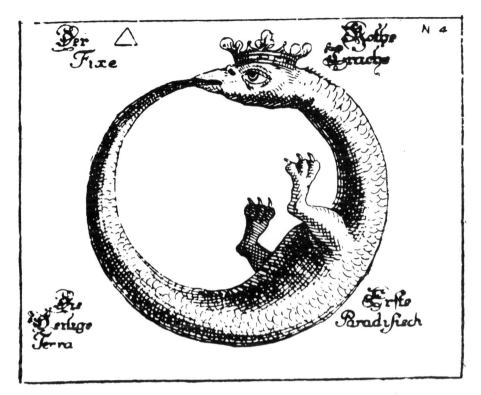

The crowned dragon as *Ouroboros*, symbol of the four elements,
from Abraham Eleazar's *Uraltes Chymisches Werk*, Leipzig, 1760

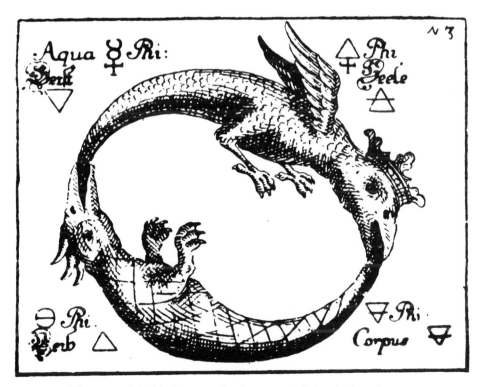

The crowned double-dragon as *Ouroboros*, symbolizing the four elements,
from Abraham Eleazar's *Uraltes Chymisches Werk*, Leipzig, 1760

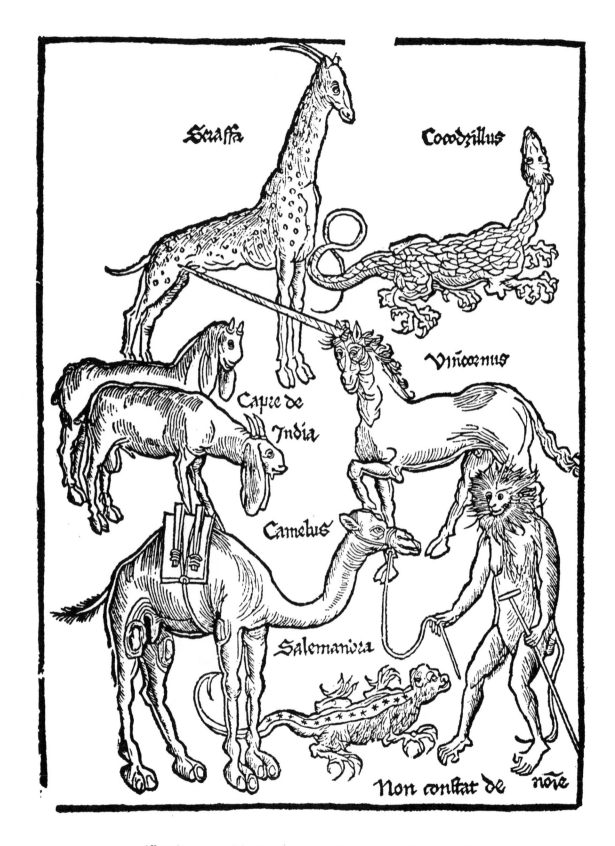

Alleged monsters of the Holy Land, from Bernhardus de Breydenbach's
Reise ins Heilige Land, printed by Petrus Drach, Speyer, 1495

Chapter 4

TERRESTRIAL MONSTERS

Besides dragons and serpents many composite monsters infested the mountains and plains, forests and jungles of every continent of the globe. Among them were the classical watchdog of Hades, the three-headed *Cerberus,* with a dragon's tail and a neck bristling with serpent heads, who lived on the shore of the Styx and prevented the shades of the dead from leaving the underworld; the fire-breathing monster *Chimera,* with the head of a lion, the body of a goat, and the tail of a serpent, who ravaged the Lycian plains in ancient Greece; and the *werewolves* or wolf-men, known to the ancient Greeks and Romans, who were human beings transformed by witchcraft and black magic into carnivorous beasts, like the French *Loup-Garou,* that roamed the plains and forests of the European lands at night. The latter existed in many forms in many other lands: as werewolves to the North American Indians; as jaguar-men in South America; as were-tigers in India, Borneo, Western Asia, China and Japan; as werelions in Africa; and in still different guises elsewhere. Many other legendary carnivorous monsters were reported in medieval natural histories: the *Lamia,* who fed on lost children; the ferocious *Manticora;* the terrifying *Basilisk,* or *Cockatrice;* and the *Gorgon,* or *Catoblepas;* as well as equally frightful creatures who were probably fanciful, imaginary representations of real but little-known beasts, such as the tiger, the hyena, the lion, wild dogs and cats of all kinds, as they first appeared to wondering and fearful eyes.

Werewolf, from Comestor's *Historica Scholastica,*
a 13th-century bestiary manuscript

Bellerophon on Pegasus, slaying the Chimera, symbol of the impossible,
after an ancient Greek vase painting

Hercules capturing the three-headed *Cerberus*, watchdog of the Gates of Hades,
symbol of guardianship (Greco-Roman mythology)

Dogue d'angleterre (English werewolf),
from Boaistuau's *Histoires prodieuses*, Paris, 1597

The Mystic Dog, from Edward Topsell's *A History
of Four-Footed Beasts*, London, 1658

The Lamia, from Edward Topsell's *A History of Four-Footed Beasts*,
printed by E. Cotes, London, 1658

The Gorgon, or Catoblepas, from Edward Topsell's *A History of Four-Footed Beasts*,
printed by E. Cotes, London, 1658

THE MANTICORA

The *Manticora* is believed to be a vampiric, man-killing monster of ancient Tataric origin, whose name derives from the Persian *martya* — man, and *xvar* — to eat. It was first mentioned in the writings of the Greek physician and natural historian Ktesias, who lived and worked at the ancient Persian court in the fifth century B.C. The existence of the Manticora was also accepted by the influential Greek philosopher Aristotle (384-322 B.C.). From that time on, the Manticora haunted ancient bestiaries and, later on, medieval natural histories. The monster was variously described by different scholars, and illustrated in bestiaries according to the fantastic imagination of the reproducing artist. It was always represented, however, as a fearful composite monster the size of a horse, usually with the body and claws of a lion, or with the scaled rump of a lioness and the talons of a griffin; sometimes with a man's head with three rows of teeth in each jaw, or with the face of a horned man, or a man's head with a mane in the form of a Phrygian cap; and usually with the tail of a basilisk or a scorpion, tipped with a poisoned arrow-head, or covered with bristly spikes which could be thrown great distances with deadly accuracy. Sometimes the Manticora was equipped with dragon's wings, or with four dugs like a cow; and its voice was said to resemble the united tones of a flute and a trumpet, parodying the human voice. In other words, this terrible monster of medieval times was endowed with every fantastic or monstrous feature known. Later works suggest it derived from distorted memories of the rarely seen man-eating tiger or the carrion-feeding laughing hyena.

The Manticora monster of Tatary, a pen drawing from a bestiary manuscript,
17th century

The man-dragon Manticora, from
a bestiary manuscript, 12th century

The terrible Manticora monster, caught in the year 1530 in the Hauberg Forest, Saxonia,
from Konrad Gesner's *De quadrupedobus vivipari*, Basle, 16th century

The man-dragon Manticora, used as a device
by the printer Busdrago, Lucca, Tuscany, 1551

The man-dragon Manticora, from Edward Topsell's *A History of Four-Footed Beasts*,
printed by E. Cotes, London, 1658

Fighting Manticoras, from an engraving by an unknown master,
Middle-Rhenish, early 15th century

THE BASILISK

The *Basilisk*, or *Cockatrice*, was a noisome beast which could stare or hiss a man to death. It was an unsavory, winged reptile born of a yolkless egg laid by a cock and hatched by a toad in the warmth of a dung-heap. So deadly was its breath that it wilted all vegetation and shattered any stone it touched; its face was so horrible that the very sight of it would kill any living thing. It was considered to be the king of all serpents and reptiles, and its name was derived from the Greek *basilikos* — little king. The Cockatrice is mentioned in the Bible (Isaiah 9:11:8), and is referred to many times, either as Cockatrice or Basilisk, in English literature: by Shakespeare; by John Gay in his *Beggar's Opera;* by Shelley in his *Ode to Naples.* In the 15th century, a decrepit nine-year-old cock was tried in the public court at Basel on the charge of having laid an egg during the days of the Dog Star; the cock,

found guilty, was put to death by the official hangman. The Basilisk was described by the Roman writer and naturalist Pliny (23-79 A.D.) as living in the warm climate of Cyrenaica and the Libyan desert, fearing only the crowing of a cock and the sight of a weasel, the only animal immune to its breath and sight. Travellers crossing the desert in the first century of Christian time took along a cock and a weasel to keep Basilisks away from their camps. In pre-St. Patrick times, the Isles of Brittania (Tin Isles) were so infested with Cockatrices that nobody dared leave his home without a silver mirror in his pocket, because its own image would kill the monster. The last recorded appearance of a Basilisk was in Warsaw in the year 1587, when two girls, playing in the cellar of their house, were allegedly killed by one's breath. In heraldry the Basilisk, and its cousin, the Wivern, symbolized the "death-dealing" eye.

Basilisk, after an English bestiary manuscript,
12th century

Basilisk used as a printer's device
by Michael Furter, Basle, 1500

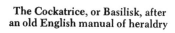

The Cockatrice, or Basilisk, after
an old English manual of heraldry

Gallo Conoda di Serpente, the Basilisk,
after A. Kircher's *Mundus Subterraneus*

Basilisk, or Cockatrice, from Johann Stabius' *De
Labyrintho*, printed by W. Huber, Nuremberg, 1510

Chapter 5

AQUATIC MONSTERS

The most superstitious group on earth are the members of the brotherhood of seafaring men, no matter what their nationality, religion, belief, creed or color. And with justification, since theirs is the only profession in which men pit their lives and limbs against all four earthly elements that endanger mankind: the churning *waters* of the oceans, fogs and rainstorms; the turbulent *air* of typhoons, hurricanes and tornados; the *terrestrial* dangers of reefs and cliffs in coastal waters; and the constant dreaded menace of *fire* on their vessels. Not to mention the possibilities of accident, hunger and thirst. No wonder that mariners of all times in all four corners of the globe, inspired no doubt by such dangerous real creatures of the deep as sharks,

sting-rays, morays, electric eels and Portuguese men-of-war — which are bad enough — populated the enormous stretches of treacherous and unsafe waters with countless forms of fictitious monsters, whose single purpose was to punish human intruders into their realm. And so they invented sea-serpents and sea-dragons, mermaids and mermen, gigantic fish and octopi, and mailed and armored sea-monsters of all kinds. And who can say with authority that somewhere in the deep crags on the ocean floor, unseen by human eyes, there do not still exist weird aquatic monsters from an antediluvian past, which might have been swept to the ocean surface in a vast upheaval, to be glimpsed by frightened sailors fighting for their lives?

Monsters of the Deep, from Sebastian Münster's
Cosmographia Universalis, Basle, 1544

Neptune riding on a Hippocampus,
from an antique Greek vase painting

Hippocampus—the Sea-horse, from Konrad Gesner's *Historiae Animalium*,
Zurich, 1551

Scylla, the sea monster living on the Italian side of the Straits of Messina
(Greco-Roman mythology)

The sea monster *Centauro-Triton,* also called *Ichthyo-Tauri*
(Greco-Roman mythology)

The Sea Devil, from a French newsletter,
printed at Gonesse, Seine-et-Oise, 16th century

The *Argus* sea monster, from Olaus Magnus' newsletter
Monstrum in Oceano Germanica (North Sea), Rome, 1537

The Crab, symbol of the sea, from a Mochica Indian design,
pre-Chimu, prehistoric Peru

The Incan crab-god of the sea,
from a Peruvian pottery decoration

The serpent-god of the sea, issuing from his shell, from an ancient
Indian ceramic decoration, San Salvador

The serpent-god of the sea, from an antique pre-Incan,
Yunca-Mochic Indian ceramic decoration, Peru

The Horned Serpent, a mythological water monster
of the Mimbreño Indians

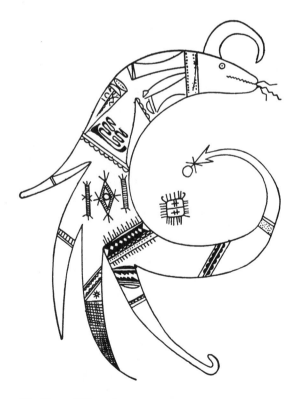

The Horned Water Serpent, a prehistoric water monster
of the Hopi Indians, Arizona

The fabled sea monster of Wasgo, from a decorative slate
engraving by the Haida Indians, British Columbia

The sea monster *Ts'um'a'ks* of the Haida Indians,
from a ceremonial tattoo, British Columbia

The Sea Grisly Monster, from a decorative drawing
by the Tlingit Indians, Wrangell, Alaska

Sea monster, from a decorative design
by the Tlingit Indians, Hetta Inlet, Alaska

Sea monster from a decorative drawing
by the Tlingit Indians, Hetta Inlet, Alaska

Kappa, the Tortoise Boy, a mischievous spirit of the rivers, part tortoise,
part monkey, who drowns swimming children (Japanese folklore)

The Giant Cat Fish, living at the bottom of the sea under Japan,
whose movements are the cause of earthquakes (Japanese folklore)

Yu-Lung, the fish-dragon monster,
from an old Chinese brush drawing.

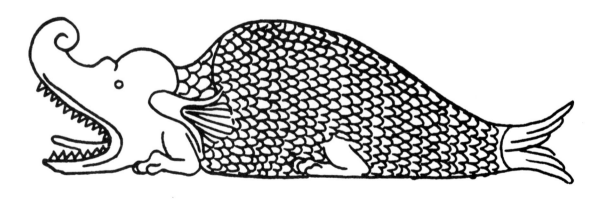

The sea monster *Makara* — Spirit of the Sea, the vehicle of Varuna,
god of the cosmos (Vedic mythology)

THE SEA SERPENT

Sea serpents are the most widely-publicized monsters of the deep. From the time of the Biblical sea monster *Nahas* (Amos 9:3), the Arabian sea serpent *Tinnin,* the serpents of Neptune who killed Laocoön in Greek mythology, and the *Midgard* serpent of Norwegian legend, this creature has cropped up time and again throughout the centuries. There are sea serpents in Hindu mythology and Fijian legend; they have been seen off the Libyan Coast, as recorded by Aristotle; in the Swedish Sea (Baltic); in the Sea of Darkness (Atlantic); off the Isle of Skye; in the Norwegian fjords; and, according to Laplandic sagas, in the Sea of Finland. Sea serpents are reported in the works of Olaus Magnus, Aldrovandus, Pontoppidan, the Bishop Hans Egede, and many others. Records of encounters with sea serpents are found in the log books of numerous ships, such as *H.M.S. Daedalus* (South Atlantic, 1848); *H.M.S. Pauline* (off Cape San Roque, 1875); the barque *Georgina* (1877); *H.M. Yacht Osborne* (off Sicily, 1877); the American ship *Sacramento* (1877); the *Samatra* (Red Sea, 1877) and the British ship *Privateer* (off Brest, 1879). Sea serpents were reported seen from the pier off Llandudno (1882); from the steamer *Sultan* (1909;) by the French mail steamer *Pacifique* (near the Loyalty Islands, 1923), and so on. There were also landlocked sea monsters, like the Ready sea serpent of Provincetown (seen 1886), and the star performer of them all, allegedly seen by thousands of visitors, *Nessy,* the sea serpent of Loch Ness in Scotland's West Highlands. Notwithstanding the manifold appearances of this monster species, however, scientists have never been able to capture a single specimen.

The water serpent of the Nile, *Hydrus,* swallowing a flying snake,
from a bestiary manuscript, 12th century

Sea serpent and dolphin, from Gaius Plinius the Elder's *Historia Naturale*,
printed by M. Sessa & P. di Ravani, Venice, 1516

Sea serpent in the Sea of Darkness, from Olaus Magnus' *Historia de Gentibus Septentrionalibus*,
printed by J. M. de Viottio, Bologna, 1555

SERPENT MARIN.

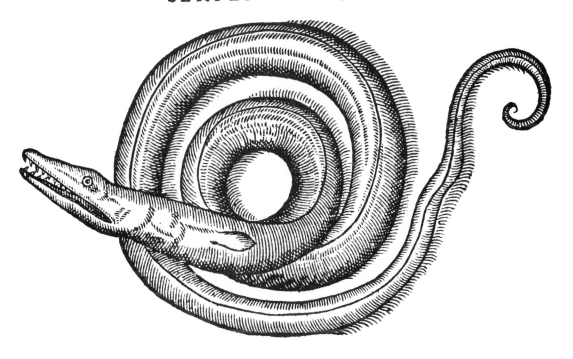

Serpent Marin — the sea serpent, from Mattioli's
Commentaires, Lyons, 1579

Sea serpent, from Bishop Hans Egede's *The New Survey of Old Greenland*,
London, 1734

Chapter 6

DENIZENS OF THE DEEP

In the folklore of seafaring people there exists a semi-human population of the deep as widespread and farflung as the travel range of the ships which ply the Seven Seas. There has never been a time in nautical history, never a country by the sea, never a harbor on the globe, in which mariners have not told of mermaids and mermen they have themselves encountered or heard about from reliable mates. Among these watery creatures were the sea and fish gods of antiquity, with their entourage of *Tritons, Nereids* and *Naiads;* the *Sirens* of Greco-Roman mythology; the Medieval *Undines;* the legendary *Melusines* of French folklore; the *Lorelei* (from the High German *lur* — to lurk, and *lai* — the rock) of Rhenish folk-saga; the *Morgans* (from the Welsh *Mari Morgan* — seafolk of Brittany) of Welsh-Bretonic folk-lore; the *Ningyos* — mermaids of Japanese mythology; and all their manifold counterparts in other Western or Oriental fables. Since the time of the ship *Argo* of Greek mythology, there seem always to have been mermaids and mermen around to lure unsuspecting sailors and their ships to destruction and a watery grave. Even in our highly technical and scientific age, no number of negative statements by scientists and natural historians, based on no matter what amount of research in submarines and bathyspheres, will ever be able to destroy the belief of superstitious mariners in the existence of these semi-human denizens of the deep. Mermaids and mermen will no doubt be riding the waves and sitting on reefs and rocks concocting their mischief for as long as there are men who go down to the sea in ships.

Mermaid and merman of the Nile Delta,
from Ulysses Aldrovandus' *Historia Monstrorum*

Melusine, from the publisher's poster for *Meluzyne*,
the fable of the beautiful mermaid, printed by Gerhard Leeu, Antwerp, 1491

Double-tailed Spanish siren, printed
by Juan Joffre, Valencia, 1520

Mermaid, from a 16th century natural history,
printed in Germany, 1558

Siren, by C. Corvinus for Sigmund Feyerabend,
Frankfort/M., 1579

The Siren of the Philosophers, from Basil Valentin's
L'Asoth des philosophes, Paris, 1659

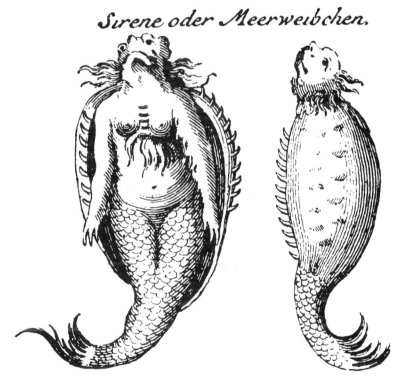

Siren, after Barbot, from *Allgemeine Historie der Reisen zu Wasser und zu Lande,*
Germany, 1747

Melusines, from Abraham Eleazar's *Uraltes Chymisches Werk*,
Leipzig, 1760

Morgan of the Black Rock, near Liverpool,
from *The Wonder of Wonders*, an English chap-book, 18th century

Ningyo, the mermaid of Japan,
from an old Japanese pen drawing

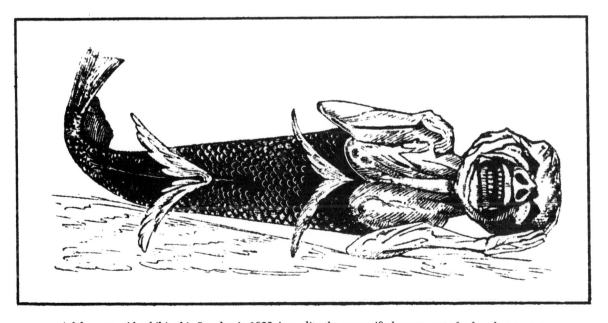

A fake mermaid exhibited in London in 1822, in reality the mummified upper part of a female orang-utan
grafted to a stuffed salmon. From a contemporary exhibition handbill

Dagon, the Philistine-Assyrian god of earth and agriculture,
half man and half fish

Triton, soother of the waves, the double-fish-tailed sea deity
of Greek mythology

The Monk-fish, a sea monster caught in 1572,
from J. Sluper's *Omnium fere gentian*, 1572

The Bishop-fish, a sea monster seen in 1531,
from J. Sluper's *Omnium fere gentian*, 1572

The Sea-king, a fanciful representation of a human-headed monster fish,
from J. W. Schmuck's *Fasculi*, 1679

The Negro-fish, caught in 1549 in the Baltic Sea, from Conrad Lycosthenes'
Prodigiorum ac ostentorum chronicon, Basle, 1557

Merman, after Rodeletius, 1554

Chapter 7

AERIAL MONSTERS

In addition to dragons and flying serpents, many other kinds of composite aerial monsters filled the skies of ancient mythology and medieval folklore. Among them were the winged gods of Assyrian-Babylonian mythology; the winged horses, lions, bulls and other creatures of Babylonia, Assyria, Egypt and Persia; the Greco-Roman flying beasts — the *Gorgons* and *Harpies;* the many bird monsters of American and Asiatic origin, such as the *Rukh,* or *Roc,* a fabulous, gigantic bird of prey of Persian-Arabic legend, so strong it could carry off the largest animals to its nest to feed its young; the *Thunderbird* of the North and South American Indians, also known to many Asiatic tribes — a supernatural eagle who created thunder by flapping its wings, and lightning by opening and closing its eyes; the eagle-men of the Amer-indians; the *Tengu* of Japanese folklore, a flying demon, half man, half bird; and the winged thunder-god *Lai Kung* of Chinese mythology. There are also semi-dragon birds such as the Japanese *Hai Riyo;* the Chinese *P'eng-niao;* the Vedic bird-king *Garuda,* vehicle of Vishnu and implacable enemy of serpents; *Make-Make,* the Easter Island bird-creator of the universe; and many a monster bird on Java and other Pacific islands. In our modern, technological age we have no need for all these aerial composite monsters of bygone times. We create our own figments of anxiety: flying saucers with their cargoes of little green men, giant ants, and robotniks.

Nisroch, the eagle-headed god
(ancient Assyrian mythology)

Marduc, the winged god of creation
(ancient Babylonian mythology)

Hippogryph, half horse, half griffin,
from a 17th century Italian signet

Hippalectryon, the cock-horse,
from an antique Greek vase painting

Senmurv, the seed-scatterer
(Sassanian-Persian mythology)

Lamussa, Assyrian-Babylonian winged lion with a human head,
ancient Babylonia

Harpy, female aerial monster of Greek mythology,
from a 16th century German bestiary

Shedu, Assyrian-Babylonian winged bull with a human head,
ancient Babylonia

The Winged Lion of St. Mark, designed by Lucas Cranach the Elder,
from *Wittemberber Heiligthumbuch*, Wittenberg, 1509

The Gorgon monster, from an antique
Greek vase painting

The Eagle Man, copper plate artifact of the
prehistoric mound builders, Etowah Mound, Georgia

The monster-bird which devours men, from a prehistoric
petroglyph (rock drawing) in the Pisa Creek River, Illinois

The Flying Eagle Man,
war god of the Zuni Indians

The flying monster-god of war
of the Inca Indians, Peru

The Eagle Man monster
of the ancient Mimbreño Indians

The bird-monster-god of the
Nasca Indians

Tengu, the mischievous aerial monster
of Japanese folklore

Hai Riyo, the ancient Japanese dragon-bird,
from a drawing in the Chi-on-in monastery, Kyoto

Lei-kung, the Chinese god of thunder,
from an old Chinese pen drawing

Garuda, king of the birds, vehicle
of Vishnu, Vedic mythology

Make-Make, the creator, seabird god
of the Easter Islands

Javanese dragon-bird, from a
shadow play puppet, Java

THE GRIFFIN

One of the oldest legendary aerial monsters is the *Gryphus, Gryphon,* or *Gryps,* whose name derives in every language from the Greek *grypos* — hooked — because of its large beak. It is called *Griffin* in English, *Griffon* in French, *Grifo* in Italian, and *Greyff* in German. It was believed to be a ferocious monster of enormous height who fed live humans to its young. Half lion, half eagle, it was so large that one could make drinking vessels from its claws. It dwelt in the country between the Hyperboreans, the North-wind people of Mongolia, and the Arimaspians, the one-eyed tribe of Scythia. It was known to the Sumerians in 3000 B.C. under the name of *Chumbaba,* and we find it also in the mythological artifacts of the Sumerians, Assyrians, Babylonians, Chaldeans, Egyptians, Myceneans, Indo-Iranians, Syrians, Scythians, and Greeks. It was mentioned in the writings of the Greek philosopher, naturalist and historian *Ktesias,* who lived at the Persian Court from 416 to 399 B.C. The monster was a sworn enemy of horses and constantly at war with the Arimaspians, who tried to capture the gold hoard guarded by the griffins. In ancient astrology, the chariot of the sun was drawn by a pair of griffins. Wherever they appeared in legend, they were always guardians of treasures, as in Iranian, Scythian and Indian mythology. Since the days of the Crusades (11th to 13th centuries) we can find the griffin in the heraldry of every nation in the West, as a symbol of eternal vigilance.

The oldest known representation of *Chumbaba* — the griffin, from an antique cylinder seal, found at Susa, Western Iran, 3000 B.C.

Griffins, from an antique Persian gold armlet,
found on the banks of the Amu-Dar'ya River, Western Asia (U.S.S.R.)

Assyrian griffin, from an antique stone carving
in the Nimrud Palace at Nineveh

Griffin used as an antique Greek *akrotrion*
(apex statuette)

Griffin killing a boar, from a 12th-century bestiary manuscript

Griffin seal of Count Friedrich von Brene,
Germany, 1208

Griffin seal of Prince Borwin von Rostock,
Germany, 1237

Griffin, after a pen drawing from a medieval German manuscript

Griffin, designed by the Master
of the Hausbuch, Germany

Greyff — the griffin, ink drawing, designed by
Hans Burgkmair

Griffin, from Sir John Mandeville's *Itinerarius*,
printed by Johann Schönsperger, Augsburg, 1482

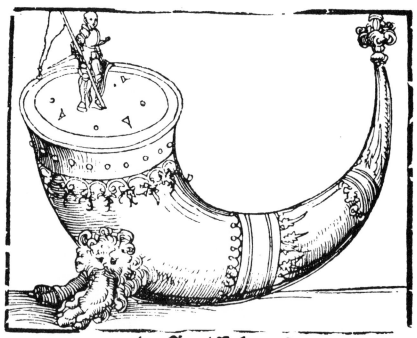

e in Greiff clawē

Silver-mounted claw of a *Greiff*, from Lucas Cranach the Elder's
Wittemberger Heiligthumbuch, Wittenberg, 1509

Greyff, designed by Albrecht Dürer, from *Emperor Maximilian's
Triumphal Arch*, printed in 1515

Griffin, from an Italian
heraldic manual, 15th century

Griffin coat of arms of the
Italian city of Perugia, 1483

Griffin from a French heraldic
manual, printed about 1581

Gryphon, from a French signet,
printed in Lyons, 1533

Griffin, from Basil Valentin's alchemic volume *Vom Grossen Stein*,
printed at Leipzig, 1601

Chapter 8

MALIGNED ANIMALS

There are many harmless animals who were maligned in bygone times as hellish monsters, such as the *Ichneumon,* a member of the weasel family, native to Africa, believed to be a super-poisonous monster because it feeds on such tidbits as snakes, rats and crocodile eggs; the *Bat* and the *Owl,* two nocturnal creatures who were considered the steady companions of witches and warlocks; the *Toad,* symbolic of death and decay; and the *Bouc Noir* (black he-goat), alleged to be the incarnation of the devil and the vehicle of witches for their trip to the Witches' Sabbath. Nearly every animal on land, in the sea or in the air, of great size or grotesque form, of nocturnal or unusual behavior, unpleasant sound or smell, has been maligned as a creature from hell; a man-killing, crop- and cattle-destroying or ship-wrecking monster; a symbol of mischief; a demonic emblem of death, the devil or hell; an instrument of black magic; or an omen of all kinds of catastrophic or otherwise unpleasant occurrences. There were also the harmless *Salamander,* supposed to live in fire; the equally harmless *Hedgehog,* accused of eating the crops stored by farmers and of milking their sleeping cows dry on nocturnal forays; the iron-eating *Ostrich,* who robbed horses of their iron shoes; the large sea mammals of the whale and seal families, accused of man-killing and ship-wrecking, *ad infinitum.*

Ichneumon, an actual African snake-killer, from an exhibition poster,
printed by Nicolaus Waldt, Strassburg, about 1580

THE WHALE

The *Whale* is the largest living sea-mammal, feeding on microscopic *plankton,* the smallest organisms in the ocean. Because of its enormous size, this completely harmless animal has been slandered throughout human history as a vicious, man-eating sea monster — from the Biblical whale who swallowed the Hebrew prophet Jonah in punishment for disobeying God, to the white whale monster *Moby Dick* in Herman Melville's American folk saga (1851). The Killer Whale was believed to be a man-killing sea monster by the Northwest American Indians and the Siberian Eskimos all along the Alaskan Coast, on the Fox and Aleutian Islands, around the Bering Sea, and in the Hudson Bay area. The hunt and capture of a killer whale amounted to a religious rite among these Indian and Eskimo tribes, from the *Nootka* Indians of Washington to the *Chuckchee* Eskimos of Siberia. They depicted the killer whale in many monstrous forms in their ceremonial art works. Whale hunting was closely interwoven with shamanistic rituals during the whaling season, which was in the early summer months. The capture and killing of a whale was celebrated with ceremonial dances, music and songs of rejoicing, feasting, and victory games, and ended in a three day mourning period to placate the evil spirit of the slain monster. Today the whale is considered a symbol of magnitude.

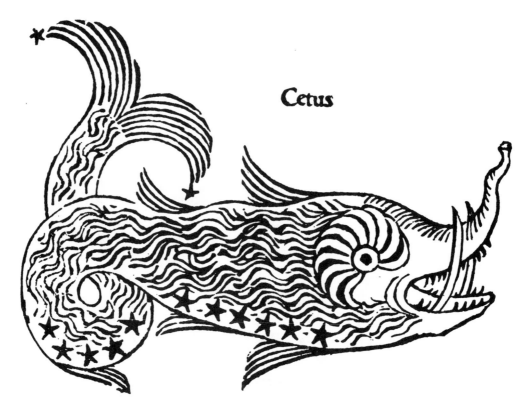

Cetus

Cetus, the mythological Greek whale-monster slain by Perseus, as a constellation, from Hyginus' *Poeticon Astronomicon*, printed at Venice, 1482

The whale swallowing Jonah, after a pen drawing in a
medieval Bible manuscript (Jonah 1:17)

Plyseter, or *Whirlpoole,* the Blower Whale, from Ulysses Aldrovandus'
Opera Omnia, printed at Bologna (1599-1668)

Beached whale-monster, from Olaus Magnus' *Historia de Gentibus Septentrionalibus*,
printed by J. M. de Viottio, Rome, 1532

The whale-monster and its young, from Konrad Gesner's
Historiae Animalium, printed at Zurich, 1551

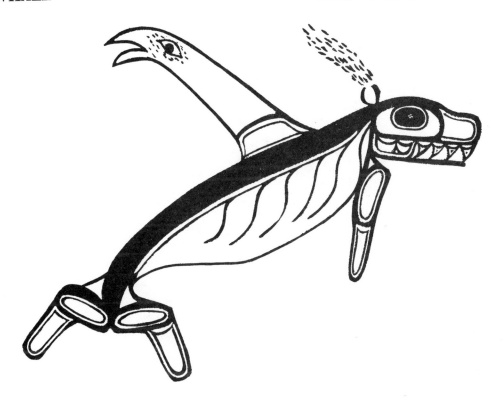

The Killer Whale, from a decorative drawing
by the Tlingit Indians, Wrangell, Alaska

The Killer Whale, from a decorative drawing
by the Haida Indians, British Columbia

THE OCTOPUS

One of the most grotesque creatures in the sea is the *Octopus*, or *Eightfoot*, whose name was derived from the Greek *octo* — eight, and *pous* — foot. It was considered by the ancient mariners to be one of the most frightening terrors of the sea. In reality, it is a small-to-large, harmless mollusk, a member of the cuttlefish family, with a soft sack-like body, a large head with a mouth on the undersurface, and eight arms covered with suckers. Its largest specimen is the *Octopus punctatus*, which lives on the ocean bottom off the Pacific Coast of North America and reaches a span of about 14 feet from arm tip to arm tip. Many a tale was told in bygone times about giant octopi that infested the farflung sea lanes. They were thought to have been able to pull whole ships with their crews to a watery grave — as in the saga of the *Kraken*, a fabulous composite monster of Norwegian sea lore, imagined as a gigantic octopus-crab rising in the *Oceanus Germanicum* (North Sea). It had an enormous, flat shape, said to be a mile and a half in circumference, and when it submerged, its many arms created a whirlpool that sucked down even the largest ships. To the same group of sea yarns belongs the Spanish-Portuguese fable of the phantom island *Man Satanaxio* (Satan's Hand), which rose every day from the waters of the Sea of Darkness (Atlantic), like a gigantic black hand, to scoop up passing ships and draw them down to the depths of the ocean. To the South, Central, and North American Indians the octopus and its relatives, the squid and the cuttlefish, were benevolent monsters, and were considered symbols of fecundity.

Giant octopus attacking a fisherman, after a Japanese engraving
by Hokusai (1760-1849)

The giant octopus, terror of the ancient mariners, attacking a vessel, from an old French engraving,
after a picture in the Church of St. Malo, France

The giant octopus attacking the submarine vessel *Nautilus*, from Jules Verne's
Twenty Thousand Leagues under the Sea, Paris, 1873

The *Hedgehog* was accused in medieval times of being a gluttonous animal which made nightly forays into barns to eat stored crops or suck sleeping cows dry of milk. The peasants of the Middle Ages killed it on sight. Actually, it is a valuable animal, since it devours cockroaches and other insects. Nowadays, European purveyors and manufacturers of foodstuffs use hedgehogs to help keep their premises clean.

Hedgehog destroying a farmer's crop,
from a German emblem, printed in 1470

The hedgehog, from Topsell's *A History of Four-Footed Beasts*,
London, 1658

According to the Roman naturalist and writer Gaius Pliny the Elder (23-79 A.D.), the *Salamander* was created from the spinal cord of a dead man. It was believed that this hellish creature was so deadly cold that it could live in fire. Asbestos was thought to be, not a mineral, but the hide shed by a Salamander. This animal is in reality a harmless member of the cold-blooded lizard family, useful in destroying insects.

Salamander cavorting in fire, representing the spirit of *materia prima*, from M. Majer's *Secretorum Chymicum*, Frankfort/M., 1687

The salamander, from P. A. Mattioli's *Commentaires*, Lyons, 1579

The *Sea Lion* is a maligned member of the seal family, actually a harmless, big-eared, fish-eating mammal. Like so many other large marine animals, however, it was held to be, in medieval times, a man-eating sea monster. Depicted with a humanized head and sharp claws, it was believed to kill and devour sailors who fell overboard.

Fanciful representation of a sea-lion,
after Rodelitus, 1554

The sea-lion, after Kolben, from *Allgemeine Historie der Reisen zu Wasser und zu Lande*,
Germany, 1747

The *Rosmarin* was a sea monster of evil repute living in the waters of the northern seas. It was believed that when it saw a man on shore, it pulled itself up to the top of the rocks with its enormous teeth, fell upon the hapless victim and ate him. In reality it was the *Walrus,* a massive, fierce-looking, fish-eating member of the seal family, which attacks only if disturbed in its breeding grounds.

Fanciful representation of the *Rosmarin,* or walrus, from a German engraving, 1560

The *Rosmarin,* or walrus, from Konrad Gesner's *Historiae Animalium,* printed at Zurich, 1551

The *Narwhale*, or *Sea Unicorn*, was believed to be a dangerous sea monster who drilled holes in the bottom planks of ships with its long, spiral tusk, so that the vessels would draw water and sink. It is actually a harmless sea mammal of the dolphin family, living in the icy waters of the Arctic. Its tusk was sold as unicorn horn, the wondrous cure-all held in such high esteem throughout medieval Europe.

The narwhale from Sir Thomas Herbert's *Some Yeares Travels into Africa and Asia*, printed at London, 1677

Fanciful representation of the narwhale, after Barbot, from *Allgemeine Historie der Reisen zu Wasser und zu Lande*, 1747

In medieval times the *Ostrich* was considered a monstrous bird which plucked the iron shoes off horses, and swallowed everything it laid eyes on. In medieval alchemy the name for vitriol was *Ostrich Stomach*, because it was believed that this bird had vitriolic stomach juices to digest all the odd things it swallowed. In heraldry the Ostrich was always represented as holding in its claw, or chewing, an iron horseshoe.

Heraldic representation of the ostrich, swallowing an iron horseshoe, from an old English armorial

Emblematic representation of an ostrich, holding an iron horseshoe, from Guillaume Gueroult's *Le Blason des Oyseaux*, printed by Arnoullet, Lyons, 1550

The *Sea Cow,* or *Manatee,* from its Carib-
bean name *manati,* is a large, peaceful,
aquatic mammal, a member of the whale
family, living on sea plants in the shallow
tropical waters off the South American and
West African coasts. It was believed in medieval times to be a vicious, human-headed,
man-eating relative of the mermaid.

Manatee, a prehistoric mound builders' copper plate artifact
from the Hopwell Mound, Ross County, Ohio

Fanciful representation of the manatee, from Konrad Gesner's
Historiae Animalium, Zurich, 1551

After the discovery of the New World, European naturalists published fanciful pictures and reports of a vicious new mail-clad monster called by the Indians *Aiochtochtli*, by the Spaniards *Armatum*, and by the Portuguese *Encuberato*. It was actually the shy *Armadillo* of the *Edentata* (toothless) family, which feeds on ants.

Symbolic armadillo, from
an ancient artifact, Mexico

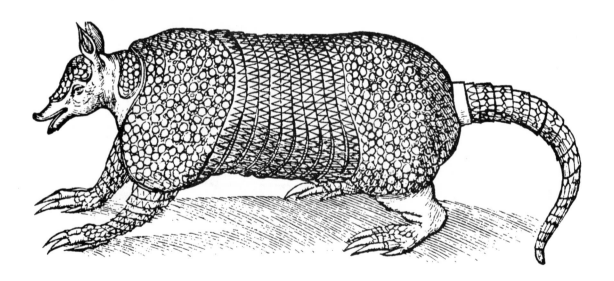

The *Ibach* (armadillo), after Nicolas Monardes, from Charles de L'Ecluse's
Simplicium medicamentorum, Antwerp, 1597

Fanciful representation of the *Su*-monster (oppossum), from André Thevet's
Singularités de la France antarctique, Antwerp, 1558

Fanciful representation of the *Haut*-monster (three-toed sloth), from André Thevet's
Singularités de la France antarctique, Antwerp, 1558

Chapter 9

BENIGN MONSTERS

Among the legendary monsters of the world were some who had no animosity toward human beings, but were, on the contrary, helpful, benevolent creatures. They appear sometimes in Western legends, but more often in those of the Far East. One of the most lovable such Oriental beasts is the *Baku* of Japanese folklore, a creature with a long, trunklike nose, patterned after a real nocturnal animal of the pachyderm family, the tapir, found in South America and the Malayan Peninsula. According to Japanese folklore the Baku lives on human dreams, and if you have a bad dream, the Baku can be willed to eat it before it becomes a nightmare. There is also the winged horse *Pegasus* of Greek mythology, symbol of poetry and the arts; the *Unicorn*, religious symbol of purity in the West, and in the East, king of the animals; the *Sphinx*, symbol of silence, with its lion's body and human head; the *Dolphin*, talisman of sailors and emblem of safe travel; the Arabian *Phoenix*, which rises from its own ashes, symbolizing resurrection and a new life after death; and the *Centaur Chiron*, a Greek mythological monster, half man, half horse, the founding father of medicine and pharmacology. These are all monstrous beings, yet friendly and helpful to humanity in one way or another. All that glitters is not gold, and neither is everything unusual or monstrous-looking necessarily terrible and fearsome. In every collection of children's fairy tales, in every land and every language, we can also find stories of dwarfs, gnomes and other friendly, man-like monsters.

The Japanese tapir, *Baku*, a nocturnal ghost animal, which feeds on bad dreams
(Japanese folklore)

THE DOLPHIN

The *Dolphin*, or *Delphinus*, was considered a kindly sea monster in antiquity, servant of the gods and helper to man. In Greek mythology it was sacred to Apollo, and was the vehicle on which the sea gods rode the waves. The ancient Greek fishermen called it *Simones* — the snubnosed — and according to the Greek naturalist Pliny, the dolphin reacted to the human voice: when fisherman called out "Simo," the dolphin came to help them spread out their nets. The best known of all dolphin legends is the Greek fable of the musician Arion who, on his return from Sicily to Corinth, was threatened with death by the crew of his ship who wanted the treasures on board. He promised to throw himself overboard if he was allowed to play his tunes once more; the sailors agreed, and a school of dolphins cavorting around the ship were so charmed by his music that when Arion leaped into the water, one of them took him on its back and brought him safe and sound into the harbor of Corinth. For this benevolent deed the gods put *Delphinus* into the sky as a constellation. It is still believed today that dolphins follow vessels to rescue passengers and crew in emergencies. In Japanese folklore the dolphin *Gregyo* — the hanging fish — is considered the best talisman against fires, and its image is placed on the roofs of houses for protection. In the West, the dolphin is an emblem of success in the arts, a messenger of good fortune, and a mascot for safe travel.

Nereid playing with a dolphin, after an antique
Greek vase painting

Neptune riding on a dolphin into the harbor of Venice, from Jacopo de Barberi's
Pianta di Venezia, printed in Venice, 1500

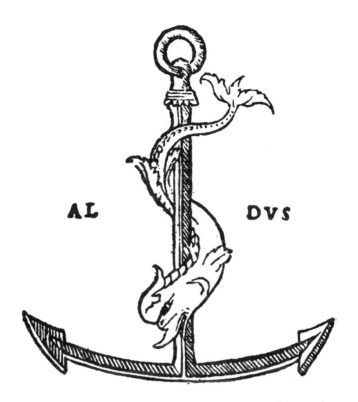

The anchor and the dolphin in the printer's device of Aldus Manutius,
the best known use of the dolphin in heraldry, Venice, c. 1500

The constellation *Al-dulfin*, or *Delphinus*,
from an early Arabic astronomical manuscript

The dolphin rescuing Arion, from the printer's
device of Johan Oporin, Basle, 1544

Fanciful dolphin amulet for safe travel,
from *The Celestial Atlas*, published in 1786

Gregyo, the hanging dolphin, used as a house charm against fire
(Japanese folk magic)

THE CENTAUR

The *Centaur*, or *Centaurus*, half man and half horse, was in Greek mythology a member of a wild and lawless race of monsters that inhabited the region of Thessaly. They were destroyed by the powerful Greek folk hero Heracles (the Roman Hercules). Only the more friendly and intelligent individuals of the race survived, like *Pholus*, an Arcadian centaur, son of Silenus, who became a friend of Heracles; and the wisest of all the centaurs, *Chiron*, son of Cronus, who was tutored by Apollo in music, and by Artemis in botanical medicine. He became the friend and physician of the gods and the teacher of the mythological heroes Heracles, Aesculapius, Jason, Achilles, Theseus, Nestor, Maleagar and the Dioscuri Castor and Pollux. When he accidentaly wounded himself with a poisoned arrow of Heracles, he was unable to die because the gods had made him immortal. To redeem him from his acute pain, the Titan Prometheus took upon himself Chiron's immortality, and the gods put the dying Chiron into the sky as the constellation Sagittarius. As the teacher of Aesculapius, Chiron was considered the founding father of medicine and pharmacology. When Francisco Pizarro landed in the New World, the natives, who had never before seen a horse or rider, fled from his mounted soldiers in the belief that they were a breed of unknown terrible monsters, half man, half beast.

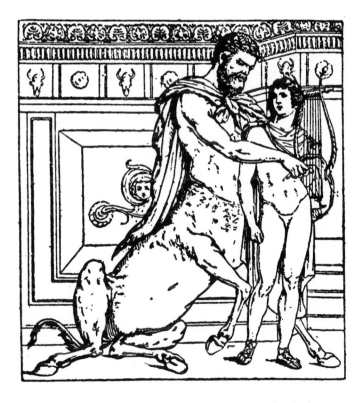

The centaur *Chiron*, teaching young Achilles to play the harp,
after an antique Roman wall painting

The centaur *Chiron*, playing with the Greek god of love, Eros,
from an old French engraving

Theseus battling the centaur, from Nicolaus Ferettus'
De structura compositionis, Forli, 1495

Young centaurs playing, from *Dialogues of Creatures Moralysed*,
London, 1520

The constellation Sagittarius, or the centaur *Archer*,
from an old French engraving of the Zodiac

THE PEGASUS

The white winged horse of ancient legend, *Pegasus,* was the most gentle of all fabled creatures. According to Greek mythology, it was believed to have been created by Poseidon from the bloody head of the slain gorgon Medusa. Caught and tamed by Athena, it became the steed of the Corinthian folk hero Bellerophon in his fight with the monster *Chimera* and in his other adventures. When Bellerophon, riding Pegasus, tried to reach the dwelling of the gods on Mount Olympus, he was thrown by the flying horse; Pegasus reached the summit alone and became the *Thundering Horse of Jove,* carrier of the divine lightning bolts. He was placed as a permanent constellation among the stars. In pre-Classical times, the figure of the sky-horse was used in astrology by the Assyrian-Babylonians, the Etruscans, the Hittites, and the early Aryans. Its name derives from the Phoenician *Pag Sus* — the bridled horse. In later tradition Pegasus became the symbolic mount of poets and artists because of the Greek legend which said that with a stamp of his hoof he caused the flow of Hippocrene, the fountain of the Muses, on Mount Helicon. Thus Pegasus became the symbol of poetic inspiration and the emblem of the creative arts. The legend of the celestial horse also reached the Far East, where it became the fabled Chinese *Kylin,* and the Japanese *Ki-Rin.*

The Babylonian Pegasus, from a wall carving,
in ancient Nineveh

Bellerophon and Pegasus, from an old Italian engraving

Pegasus and the Genie of Art, from an old French engraving

The celestial horse, *Kylin*, the Chinese version of the Pegasus,
from an old Chinese pen drawing

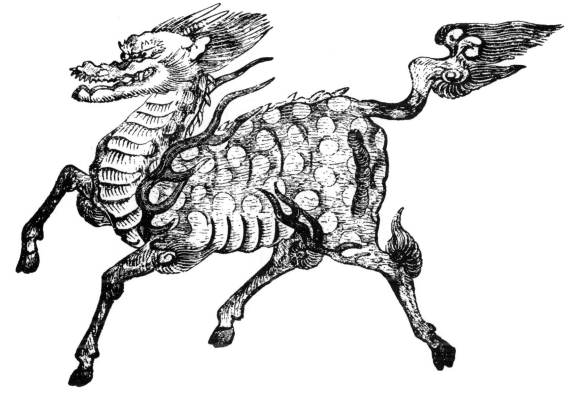

Ki-Rin, the Japanese version of the Pegasus,
from an ancient drawing in a Kyoto temple

THE PHOENIX

The *Phoenix, Fenix* or *Fire-Bird,* is believed to be of ancient Indian or Persian origin. It was called the *Bennu* in Egyptian mythology and lived in the deserts of Arabia, from where it flew every five hundred years to the holy city of Heliopolis in Egypt, to build in the Temple of the Sun a nest of myrrh, cassia and frankincense. This nest was ignited by Ra, the sun god, and consumed by fire. The cremated phoenix rose rejuvenated from its own ashes, symbolizing the undying spiritual instinct of man and the promise of reincarnation after death. The phoenix was also emblematic of life and immortality in ancient Greece and Rome. Christianity borrowed it from the Ancients as the emblem of the spirit's victory over death, the symbol of the resurrection of the soul (Job 29:18). In Far Eastern belief, the phoenix was one of the Four Mythical Animals. In Chinese mythology it was the Feng-Huang (*Feng* — the male phoenix, and *Huang* — the female), king of the feathered race, and symbol of peace and prosperity. In Chinese poetry it was the silver-breasted love-pheasant, emblem of the Empress of China, and harbinger of happiness, typifying friendship and affection. In the mythology of Japan the phoenix was the sacred bird Ho-Oo (*Ho* — the male phoenix, and *Oo* — the female), the emblem of wise and good government and a symbol of good fortune. Throughout the world, the phoenix has become an emblem of good luck, prosperity and immortality.

The *Bennu* bird, or the Egyptian phoenix,
after an antique Egyptian wall painting

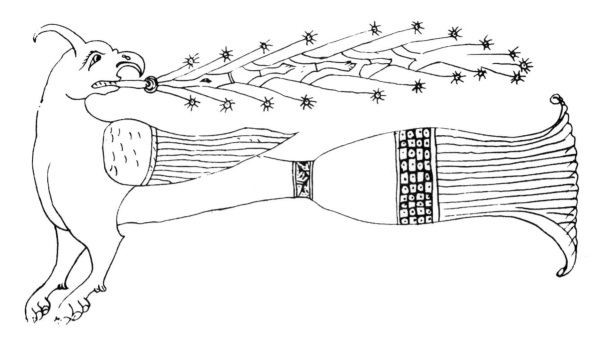

The Persian Fire-bird, from Comestor's *Historia Scholastica,*
a bestiary manuscript, 13th century

The phoenix with the ornamented cross, as the symbol of the resurrection of
Christ and eternity, from *Quattuor Evangelica,* Belgrade, 1552

The phoenix rising from its ashes, Christian symbol of resurrection,
from Boschius' *Ars Symbolica*, Augsburg, 1702

The phoenix rising from the fire, from Magister Joseph Berruerius'
Bestiarius, Savona, 1524

The silver-crested Love Pheasant, the poetic Chinese phoenix,
symbol of friendship and affection and harbinger of happiness,
from an old Chinese pen drawing

Ho-Oo, the male-female Japanese phoenix, symbol of good and wise government,
from an old Japanese pen drawing

Feng-Huang, the male-female Chinese phoenix, ruler of the feathered animals,
from an ancient Chinese pen drawing

THE UNICORN

The *Unicorn* is the most widely known of all mythical animals, appearing in one form or another in nearly all Western and Oriental mythologies. According to Biblical etiology, the unicorn became extinct because it was thrown out of the ark, and drowned. Its name derives from the Latin *unus* — one, and *cornu* — horn. It was the Biblical *Reem*, mentioned in Deuteronomy 33:17: *"his horns are like the horns of the unicorn."* In the belief of the early Christian Church, it was the symbol of virginity and the emblem of the power of love. In the sixteenth and seventeenth centuries, ground unicorn horn was a popular ingredient in European medicine and was used as a potent remedy against pestilence and poison. Unicorn horns were put on the tables of rulers and church dignitaries because it was believed that the horns would sweat at the presence of poisoned food. These horns, which sold for a king's ransom in Europe, were in reality the tusks of the narwhale. In antiquity, Ktesias and Herodotus reported the presence of unicorns in Libya and Ethiopia. Far Eastern folklore is especially rich in one-horned animals; unicorns are found in the mythologies of Tibet, Tartary, Malaya, and the Himalayan region. The most prominent of all Oriental unicorns is the *Chin-Lin*, or Dragon-Horse, the king of all animals, one of the four fabulous creatures of Chinese mythology, and the symbol of good luck, longevity, grandeur, felicity and wise administration. It appears only when a sage is about to be born, and is said to have been seen last at the birth of Confucius.

The Assyrian bull unicorn under the sacred tree of lotus buds, from an antique Assyrian stone relief

The Babylonian unicorn, from an antique wall carving at Pollidrara,
Etruria, Italy

Monocerus — the unicorn, from a bestiary manuscript,
12th century

The virgin and the capture of the unicorn, from a 12th-century bestiary manuscript

The unicorn with St. Justine and
Alphonse I of Ferrara

The Pope with the unicorn as the symbol of the Holy Ghost, from Paulus Scaliger's
Explanatio Imaginum, an emblem book, Cologne, 1570

The unicorn, from Konrad Gesner's *Historiae Animalium*,
printed at Zurich, 1551

King, the Chinese single-horned stag, from an antique Chinese pen drawing

Sz, the Sword Ox, or Malayan unicorn, from an antique Chinese pen drawing

Lu, the one-horned Chinese ass, from an ancient Chinese drawing

Ki, the Chinese male unicorn, from an antique Chinese pen drawing

Lin, the Chinese female unicorn, from an antique Chinese pen drawing

Ki-Lin, the combined male and female Chinese unicorn,
from an antique Chinese pen drawing

The Japanese unicorn, from an old Japanese pen drawing

THE SPHINX

The *Sphinx* was one of the fabulous composite beasts of Egyptian mythology, a creature with a woman's head, a bull's loins, a lion's claws, and an eagle's wings. The human head represented intelligence and knowledge; the lion's claws stood for daring and action; the bull's loins denoted stamina and perseverance; and the folded eagle's wings, silence. The sphinx was the guardian of Egyptian magic and occult wisdom, endowed with the four virtues of the Magi: knowledge, daring, will power and silence. Sphinxes were placed at the entrances of palaces and temples to guard their mysteries, and to warn those who penetrated into these sanctuaries to conceal from the profane the knowledge they had gained. Variations of sphinxes are found in many parts of the ancient world; there are three types in Egypt alone: the human-headed *Andro-Sphinx*, the ram-headed *Crio-Sphinx*, the hawk-headed *Hieraco-Sphinx*. There were also the man-headed sphinxes of Assyrian-Babylonian temples and palaces, and the oracular divinity sphinx of Thebes in Bœotia. Some existed even in Far Eastern legends. With the exception of the Greek Sphinx of Thebes (the only talking sphinx of ancient mythology), who killed passers-by who were unable to answer its riddles, all sphinxes were friendly and benevolent creatures, the guardians of religious, occult and magic secrets; and their image became the symbol of mystic wisdom and the emblem of silence in many parts of the world. The legend of the sphinx reached even faraway China, whose mythology abounded in monsters who guarded palaces of worship and protected believers at their devotions.

The Babylonian sphinx, from an antique stone carving
at the Nimrud Palace, Nineveh

The woman-headed Egyptian sphinx, from an old French engraving,
after an antique stone carving

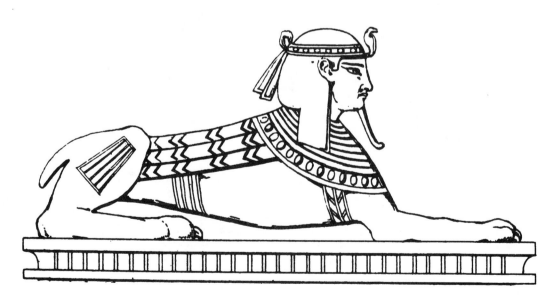

The Grecian sphinx of Thebes, after an antique stone carving

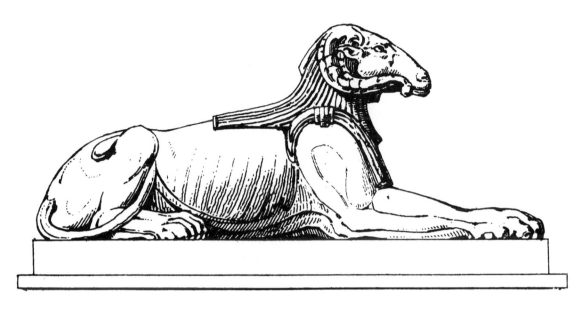

**The ram-headed Egyptian Crio-sphinx, from an old French engraving,
after an antique stone carving**

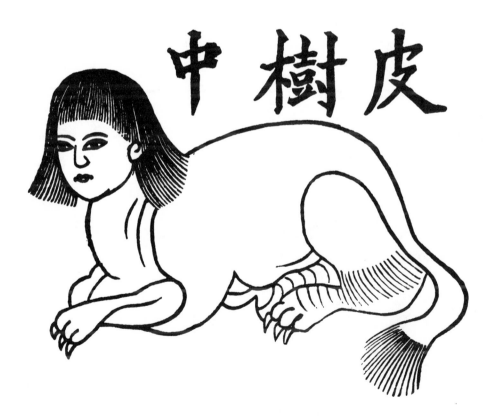

The Chinese sphinx, from an old Chinese brush drawing

Chapter 10

MEDIEVAL MARTIANS

It is an inescapable conclusion that many of the ancient explorers, physicians and scholars of natural history were the science-fiction writers of their time. The illustrations in their volumes, depicting all kinds of fanciful, wondrous people on other continents, from Ethiopia to Cathay, bear a striking resemblance to the Martians and Venusians of our modern s-f writers. Medieval geographic knowledge of far-off and unexplored places was no better than our current knowledge of planets and stars in outer space. And all these faraway lands were populated, in the reports of these scientists, by monstrous peoples, such as the *Cannibali* of the New World, the headless *Acephali*, the *Anthropophagi* and the *Musteros*, found from Libya to the Far East, the Indian *Sciopedes*, a people with hypertrophic feet, the bird-headed tribes of Africa, and

many others. Some of these were even real, and still exist today, such as the cannibalistic Indians of South America, the diminutive *Negrillo Pygmies* of Africa, and the *Negrito Dwarfs* of Asia. We have to give the scientific observers of bygone days the benefit of the doubt: their headless people with faces on their chests may have been burnoosed desert warriors; their bird- or animal-headed creatures, plumed jungle dancers or masked and painted witch doctors; their hairy wild men and women, anthropoid apes, such as orangutans or gorillas, all seen from a distance.

Modern science-fiction derived its ideas for the population of outer space directly from the medieval natural history volumes: it merely substituted steel and plastics for feathers and scales, and electronics for magic.

Musteros, Pigmei and *Sciopedi*, from Guilliano de Dati's *Il secondo Cantare dell' India*, printed by Johann Besicken & Sigismund Mayer, Rome, 1494

Monstrous people in faraway lands, from Conrad von Megenberg's *Puch der Natur*,
printed by Johann Bämler, Augsburg, 1478

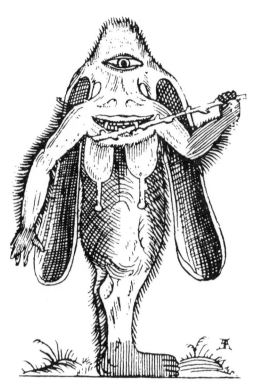

One-eyed *Cyclop* of Sicily

Simia Satyrus from India

Elephant-headed *Troglodyt* of Ethiopia

From *Curious Creatures*, by John Ashton, after Gaius Plinius Secundus

The *Cannibali* of South America,
from a quaint German broadside printed in 1505

Monsters in the German *Zauberwald* (Fairy Forest), from F. Petrarka's *Das Glücksbuch*,
designed by Hans Weiditz, printed by Heinrich Steyner, Augsburg, 1539

Acephali, the headless people of Libya,
from *Korte Wonderliche Beschryvinge*, Holland, 1563

Crane-man of Africa, from Aldrovandus'
***Opera Omnia*, printed at Bologna, 1642**

Hairy Wild Man Monster, from J. Sluper's
***Omnium fere gentian*, 1572**

Wild Man in Captivity, from Boaistuau's
Histoires prodigieuses, 1597

Wild Woman and *Pigmy* presented to the king,
from Boaistuau's *Histoires*, Paris, 1597

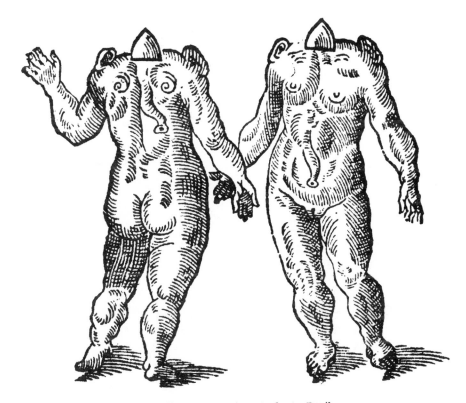

Headless monsters from Ambroise Paré's
Livres de Chirurgerie, Paris, 1573

Chapter 11

MONSTROUS MUTANTS

Our survey of monsters would be incomplete if we did not take into consideration the manifold weird stories of monstrous human and animal mutants found in the folklore and in the medical and natural history volumes of all periods. Such stories have abounded, since the days of the Greek philosopher Ktesias (5th century B.C.) at the court of the Persian ruler Artaxerxes I, and especially since the works of the Roman naturalist Gaius Plinius Secundus (23-79 A.D.), the founder of modern natural history. Medieval pitchmen collected real and faked monstrous freaks, which they sold at exorbitant prices to rulers for the entertainment of courtiers and their ladies, or exhibited profitably in cities and towns and in side shows at country fairs. In those days the manufacture of real living freaks was an extensive and flourishing business and home industry. Primitive, uneducated women of the poorer classes used all

kinds of known and long-forgotten tricks, and deliberately suffered severe injury, to bear disfigured children who could be sold for substantial sums to carnival exhibitors. Some of the monstrous creatures shown in the shops and pubs of enterprising rural tavernkeepers and city merchants were embalmed fake monsters of simian origin, to which were grafted parts of birds, fishes and reptiles. The real living freaks had their medieval make-up men who exaggerated their monstrous features by all kinds of artificial means. Chest toupees are not an invention of Hollywood, but were worn by many a hairy wild man or woman in medieval side shows long ago. Every age had its Barnum who exhibited such monsters to a gaping crowd, as long as they were willing to pay a pfenning, centime, kopeck or rupee for a shuddering look at these unfortunate creatures, with the innermost thought: *There but for the grace of God go I.*

Pig-headed Devil monster, allegedly born in 1110 at Liège,
from a pen drawing in a French occult manuscript *La Magie Noire*, France, 19th century

Deutung des Münchkalbs
zu Freiberg / Doctoris Martini
Luthers.

Monster calf, born in 1496 at Freiberg, Saxonia, called the *Monks Calf*,
from a Lutheran pamphlet, designed by Lucas Cranach the Elder, Nuremberg

Der Bapſteſel zu Rom

Monster taken from the Tiber at Rome in 1496, called the *Pope's Donkey*,
from a Lutheran pamphlet, designed by Lucas Cranach the Elder, Nuremberg

Monster pig born at Landsee in Bavaria, designed by Albrecht Dürer,
from a broadside, printed at Nuremberg, 1496

Human freaks, from Werner Rolewinck's *Les Fleurs et manières de temps passés*,
printed by Jehan le Petit and Michel le Noir, Paris, 1513

**Handbill for the exhibition of a human monster with two heads and four hands,
Berlin, 1507**

Anzeygung wunderbarlicher

geschichten vnd geburt/dises XXXI. Jars
zu Augspurg geschehen. 2c.

Zu wissen/das newlicher tag zu Augspurg ein schwangere fraw/
so zur gepurt nider kumen/drey wunderbarlicher/vnnatürlicher/
seltzamer/vngewönlichen/vnd vormals vnerhörten/noch der gleichen
vnförmlichen gestalt/gesehener früchten/auß irem leyb in dise welt ge-
boren vnd gebracht hat.

Die erst creatur vnd geburt/so auß irem leyb kumen/ist gewesen ein
ainich menschen haubt/one leyb/hende/vnd füß/in einem heütlin/oder
belglein gelegen/Wie dañ dise figur zu erkennen gibt vnd anzeygt/2c.

Die ander vnnatürlich/vngestalt geburt vnd figur vbertreffenlich
wunderbar/hat ein haubt vñ mund zugleich einem fisch/Nemlich wie
ein hecht/seinen von aller glidmaß gantzen leib/auff form vnd gleych-
nus eines Froschs/vñ vor seinem hindern/als ein Eder/einen schwantz
gehabt.

Die drit vnförmlich geburt/so von der frawen leyb komen/ist gleich
gewest einem jungen schweyn/Vnd ist dise vnd auch die andern/als
pald sie an tag komen/gestorben.

Was aber dise Monstra vnd widernatürliche früchten vnd wunder
bedeütten vnd anzeygen/das wayß allein Got im himel/Der wende
alle ding durch sein götliche barmhertzigkeit zum besten/2c.

Broadside announcement about the birth of a whole litter of monsters,
born to one woman at Augsburg, 1531

Abreissung eines vngestalten Kinds/ so am Neu=
twen Jars abent/ M. D. Lrrviij. geborn.   Auch eines vngestalten Kalbs/ von einem
Kü geworpffen/damit ein Spanier vorhinzu thun/vnd sein vnzucht getriben hat. ꝛc

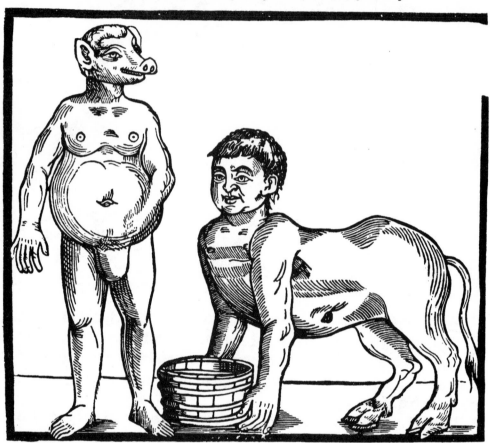

NM Abent dieses Neuwen Jaers M. D. Lrrviij. ist diese mißfellige vnd vnge=
stalte Monster eines Kindes/in dem Lande Cleeff/in ein Dorff genennet Praest geborn/in form
vnd gestalt/wie alhie vor augen zu sehen/nemblich/ mit einem Schweinßmaul/vñ einem grossen
Bauch wie ein Trum̃/darjnnen der eine handt vnd Arm inwendig vermischt vnnd ingewachsen/
an die ander Handt sechs Finger/ an beiden Füssen sechs Tehen/ ein Gemacht wie ein Blaß/ ist
gestorben auff den Newen Jars tag/ vnd heimlich begraben vnd hingestickt worden.

Diese vnd ander dergleiche Monstra vnd vngestalte Mißburten geschehen fest viel vnd allerley dieser zeit/
vnd seind nichte dann ernstlicke warnungen/ darmit alle Schwangere Frauwen verursacht mochten worden/ zu
Gott den Allmechtigern Schepffer aller Creaturen mit dem gebete/in warer Gottes fruchten stets an zuhalten/
daß er sie gnedichlich/wenn die zeit da ist/erlöse/vnd mit rechtschaffene Leibes Frucht begnaden wölle/ damit sein
heyliges Nam gelobt vnd gepreißt mocht werden.   Ist auch ein erschrecklich fürbildt allen liechtfertigen Frau=
wen/die sich dann offtmal mit Buben vnd Gesellen in vnzucht anlegen/ vñ wenn sei alß denn bekomen/darnach
sie selber geringt haben/sich vnd jhrem frucht mit grosser vngedult erschrecklich verfluchen vnd verschweren/ vnd
damit offtmal verursachen zu sulchen mißtalten geburten.

Diß ander vngestalte Kalb/ mit dem halben Leibe einem Menschen gleich/ ist vorgangener zeit im Lande
Berge/damals da die Spanier dat Stettlin Hernberg in hetten/von einem Kü geworpffen/vnd ist vielen leuten
ennlich/daß ein Spanier mit derselben Kü sein vnzucht solte gedreuen haben.

Broadside announcement about the birth of two human monsters, one with a pig's head,
the other with the hind part of a calf, Nuremberg, 1578

Broadside announcement about the birth of a sheep with one head and three bodies,
Clausenburg, Hungary, 1620

A human freak, called the *Siren of Ravenna*,
allegedly born in 1512 at Ravenna,
from Ambroise Paré's *Livres de Chirurgerie*, Paris, 1573

The figure of a Colt with a man's face.

At *Verona* Anno Dom. 1 2 5 4. a mare foaled a colt with the perfect face of a man, but all the reſt of the bodie like an horſ: a little after that, the war between the *Florentines* and *Piſans* began, by which all *Italie* was in a combuſtion.

A colt with a man's face, allegedly foaled in 1254 at Verona,
from Ambroise Paré's *Livres de Chirurgerie*, Paris, 1573

Monster boy with four arms and four legs

Monster man with parasitic boy, seen in 1530

Monster couple with two heads (after Rhodiginus)

Dog boy monster, half boy, half dog

Female twins joined at the back

Female monster with two heads

From Boaistuau's *Histoires Prodigieuses*, Paris, 1573

Woman monster, half cat, half woman

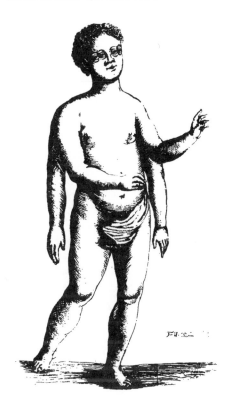

Girl monster with four eyes and arms

From J. W. Schmuck's *Fasculi*, 1679

Fish-boy born in 1684 at Beiseiglia, Italy, from an
exhibition handbill printed in England

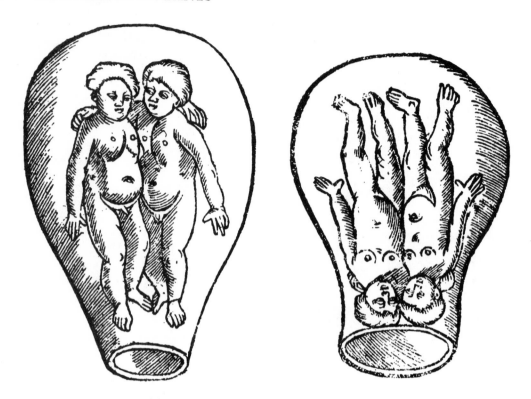

Fanciful medical representation of joined twins in the womb,
from Euchaire Rodion's *Diverse travaux et enfantemens des femmes*, printed by Nicolas Bonfons, Paris, 1577

The lion-headed Barbara Urselin, born in 1641 in Augsburg,
from Ulysses Aldrovandus' *Opera Omnia Monstrum Historia*, printed at Bologna, 1668

English boy monster, born in 1552

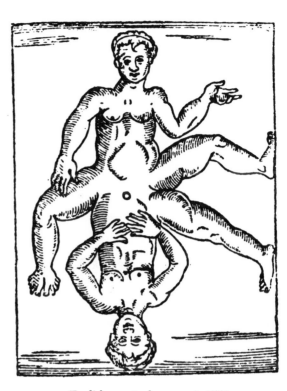

English monster boy, seen in 1554

From E. Fenton's *Secrete wonders of Nature*, printed in England, 1569

**Horrible monstrous mutant seen in Cracow,
from Lycosthenes' *Prodigiorum*, Basle, 1557**

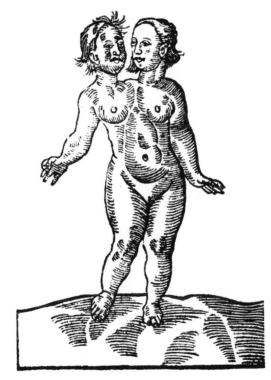

Two-headed girl mutant, from Ambroise Paré's
Livres de Chirurgerie, Paris, 1573

BIBLIOGRAPHY

ALDROVANDUS, ULYSSES, *Historia Monstrorum* (Bologna, c. 1650).

——————, *Opera Omnia* (Bologna, 1599-1668).

——————, *Serpentum et Draconium Historiae* (Bologna, 1640).

Allegemeine Historie der Reisen zu Wasser und zu Lande (Germany, 1747).

ARCHEOLOGICAL INSTITUTE OF AMERICA, *Mythology of All Races* (Boston, 1925-1936).

ASHMOLE, ELIAS, *Theatrum Chymicum Britannicum* (London, 1652).

ASHTON, JOHN, *Curious Creatures in Zoology* (New York, n.d.).

ATSUHARU, SAKAI, *Japan in a Nutshell* (Yokohama, 1949).

BARBERI, JACPO DE, *Pianta di Venezia* (Venice, 1500).

BELON, PIERRE, *Historical naturelle* (Paris, 1554).

BENWELL, GLENN & WAUGH, ARTHUR, *Sea Enchantress* (New York, 1965).

BERRUERIUS, JOSEPH, *Bestiarius* (Savona, 1524).

BLAKE, WILLIAM, *Book of Job* (London, 1825).

BOAISTUAU, PIERRE, *Histoires prodigieuses* (Paris, 1597-98).

BOSCHIUS, *Ars Symbolica* (Augsburg, 1702).

BREYDENBACH, BERNHARD VON, *Reise ins Heilige Land* (Petrus Drach, Speyer, 1495).

BRODERICK, M. & MORTON, A. ANDERSON, *A Concise Dictionary of Egyptian Archaeology* (London, 1902).

BRUNFELS, OTHMAR, *Herbarium* (Johannes Schott, Strassburg, 1530).

Das Buch Belial (Jacobus de Teramo, Augsburg, 1473).

BUDGE, E. A. WALLIS, *The Nile* (Cairo, 1912).

BUNYAN, JOHN, *The Holy War made by Shaddai upon Diabolus* (Dorman Newman and Benjamin Alsop, London, 1682).

The Celestial Atlas (1786).

CHAMPOLLION-FIGEAC, *L'Univers Pittoresque* (Firmin Didot Frères, Paris, 1848).

CLEMENT, CLARA ERSKINE, *A Handbook of Legendary and Mythological Art* (Boston, 1879).

Codex Marcianus (Venice, 11th century).

COLUMNA, FRANCISCUS, *Hypnerotomachia Poliphili* (Aldus Manutius, Venice, 1499).

COMESTOR, PETRUS, *Historia Scholastica* (13th century).

CRANACH THE ELDER, LUCAS, *Wittemberger Heiligthumbuch* (Wittenberg, 1509).

Dialogues of Creatures Moralysed (London, 1520).

DATI, GIULIANO DE, *Il secondo Cantare dell'India* (Johann Besicken & Sigismund Mayer, Rome, 1494).

EGEDE, Bishop HANS, *The New Survey of Old Greenland* (London, 1734).

ELEAZAR, ABRAHAM, *Uraltes Chymisches Werk* (Leipzig, 1760).

FEIL, V., *Vögelin Praktik* (Hans Singriener, Vienna, 1534).

FENTEN, E., *Certaine Secrete wonders of Nature* (London, 1569).

FERETTUS, NICOLAUS, *De structura compositionis* (Forli, 1495).

FLOURY, PHIL., *Compendiosa* (Jean Meurausse, Paris, 1510).

GESNER, KONRAD, *De quadrupedobus vivipari* (Basle, 16th century).

KIRCHER, ATHANASIUS, *Mundus Subterraneus* (17th century).

——————————, *Oedipus Aegyptiacus* (Rome, 1652).

LAYARD, AUSTEN HENRY, *Discoveries in Nineveh and Babylon* (New York, 1853).

——————————, *Nineveh and its Remains* (London, 1849).

LEACH, MARIA & FRIED, JEROME, *Dictionary of Folklore, Mythology and Legend* (New York, 1949).

L'ECLUSE, CHARLES DE, *Simplicium medicamentorum* (Antwerp, 1597).

LEEU, GERHARD, *Meluzyne* (Antwerp, 1491).

LICETUS, FORTUNA, *De Monstrorum Natura* (Padua, 1634).

LYCOSTHENES, CONRAD, *Prodigiorum ac ostentorum chronicon* (Henri Petri, Basle, 1557).

La Magie noire (Paris, 19th century).

——————————, *Historiae Animalium* (Zurich, 1551).

——————————, *Icones Animalium* (Zurich, 1560).

GODDARD, PLINY EARL, *Indians of the Northwest Coast* (New York, 1924).

GOULD, CHARLES, *Mythical Monsters* (London, 1886).

GUBERNATIS, ANGELO DE, *Mythologie zoologique, ou les légendes animales* (Paris, 1874).

GUEROULT, GUILLAUME, *Le Blason des Oyseaux* (Arnoullet, Lyons, 1550).

GUISIUS, MATTHAEUS, *Dialogy* (Switzerland, 1521).

HERBERT, THOMAS, *Some Yeares Travels into Africa and Asia* (London, 1677).

Hermaphrodisches Sonn- und Mondskind (Mainz, 1752).

HORAPOLLO, *Selecta Hierogryphica* (Rome, 1597).

HOWEY, M. OLDFIELD, *The Encircled Serpent* (New York, 1955).

HYGINUS, *Poeticon Astronomicon* (Erhard Ratdolt, Venice, 1482).

JAMSTHALER, H., *Viatorium Spagyricum* (Frankfort/M., 1625).

MAGNUS, OLAUS, *Monstrum in Oceano Germanica* (Rome, 1573).

——————————, *Historia de Gentibus Septentrionalibus* (J. M. de Viottio, Bologna, 1555).

MAJER, M., *Secretorum Chymicum* (Frankfort/M., 1687).

MANDEVILLE, Sir JOHN, *Itinerarius* (Johann Schönsperger, Augsburg, 1482).

MATTIOLI, PIERRE ANDRE, *Commentaires* (Guillaume Roville, Lyons, 1579).

MEAD, CHARLES W., *Old Civilizations of Inca Land* (New York, 1924).

MEGENBERG, CONRAD VON, *Puch der Natur* (Johann Baemler, Augsburg, 1478).

MULLER, NIKLAS, *Glauben, Wissen und Kunst der Alten Hindus* (Florian Kupferberg, Mainz, 1822).

MUNSTER, SEBASTIAN, *Cosmographia Universalis* (Basle, 1544).

——————————, *De Africae regionibus* (Basle, 16th century).

MURRAY, ALEXANDER S., *Manual of Mythology* (New York, 1954).

Das Neue Testament, designed by Hans Burgkmair (Silvan Othmar, Augsburg, 1523).

PARE, AMBROISE, *Des monstres tans terrestes* (Paris, 1573).

PLINIUS SECUNDUS (MAJOR), GAIUS, *Historia Naturalis* (M. Sessa & P. Di Ravani, Venice, 1516).

——————————, *The Natural History of*—— (Translated into English by Philemon Holland, 1601. Reprinted, New York, 1964).

Quattuor Evangelica (Belgrade, 1552).

RENALDINI, PANFILO DI, *Innamorata Ruggeretto* (Comin de Trino do Monferrato, Venice, 1555).

ROBBINS, ROSSELL HOPE, *The Encyclopedia of Witchcraft and Demonology* (New York, 1959).

RODION, EUCHAIRE, *Des diverse travaux et enfantemens des femmes* (Nicolas Bonfons, Paris, 1577).

ROLEWINCK, WERNER, *Les fleurs et manières de temps passés* (Jehan le Petit et Michel le Noir, Paris, 1513).

SCALIGER, PAULUS, *Explanatio Imaginum* (Cologne, 1570).

SCHENK, J. G., *Monstrorum Wunderbuch* (Germany, 1610).

SCHMUCK, J. W., *Fasculi* (1679).

SELIGMAN, KURT, *Mirror of Magic* (New York, 1948).

SEYFFERT, OSKAR, *Lexicon der klassischen Alterthumskunde* (Leipzig, 1882).

SLUPER, J., *Omnium fere gentian* (1572).

Speculum humanae salvationis (Günther Zainer, Augsburg, 1473).

SPENSER, EDMUND, *The Faerie Queene* (William Ponsonby, London, 1590).

STABIUS, JOHANN, *De Labyrintho* (W. Huber, Nuremberg, 1510).

THEVET, ANDRE, *Singularités de la France Antarctique autrement nommé Amérique* (Christopher Plantin, Antwerp, 1558).

THOMPSON, C. J. S., *The Mystery and Lore of Monsters* (New York, 1931).

A Timely Warning to Rash and Disobedient Children (Edinburgh, 1721).

TOPSELL, EDWARD, *A History of Four-Footed Beasts* (E. Cotes, London, 1658).

VALENTIN, BASIL, *L'Asoth des philosophes* (Paris, 1659).

——————————, *Vom Grossen Stein* (Leipzig, 1601).

VERNE, JULES, *Twenty Thousand Leagues under the Sea* (Paris, 1873).

WILLIAMS, C. A. S., *Outlines of Chinese Symbolism* (Peiping, 1931).

The Wonder of Wonders, (England, 18th century).

GLOSSARY

ABRAXAS The serpent-legged god of magical influence.

ANDRO-SPHINX The human-headed sphinx of Egypt.

AMPHISBAENA A reptile with a head at both ends which can walk in either direction; according to Pliny, wearing a live amphisbaena is a safeguard in pregnancy, a dead one a remedy for rheumatism.

ARGUS In Greek mythology the giant with a hundred eyes; after he was killed by Hermes, his eyes were put in the tail of the peacock; today Argus is a name for an alert watchman.

ASOOTEE In Hindu mythology the serpent with its tail in its mouth encircling the three parts of the universe.

AZON In Persian mythology the sun god of creative motion, symbolized by the serpentine wheel of the Spirit of Life.

BAKU A nocturnal dream-eating tapir of Japanese lore which could be willed to eat one's bad dreams.

BASILISK or COCKATRICE A fabulous serpent monster which tracked crocodiles and ate their eggs; its image was extensively used in heraldry.

BEHEMOTH A giant Biblical land monster, variously thought of as a large hippopotamus or gigantic water buffalo; today denoting anything exceptionally large of its kind.

BENNU The heron-like sacred bird of Egyptian mythology, emblem of resurrection.

BOAS An enormous serpent living on the Italian mainland in the 1st century A.D. which was believed to suck the milk of sleeping cows and feed on small children.

BOUC NOIR A black he-goat alleged to be the incarnation of the devil and the vehicle of witches for their trip to the Witches Sabbath.

CATOBLEPAS or GORGON An iron-clad bull monster that lived on the islands of Gorgates and fed on deadly shrubs and poisonous herbs. Its horrible breath was reputed to kill every attacker instantly.

CECROPS The first king of Attica, half man, half serpent, who established himself on the Acropolis and founded the township of Cecropia.

CENTAUR In Greek mythology a member of a wild and lawless race of monsters, half man and half horse, that inhabited the region of Thessaly.

CERBERUS The three-headed watchdog of Greek and Roman mythology who guards the gates of Hades.

CETUS The Whale constellation, celestial reincarnation of the Greek mythological sea-monster sent by Poseidon to devour Andromeda.

CHEN-LUNG A dragon of Chinese lore that guards from the eyes of mortals the wealth concealed in the earth's interior.

CHIMERA A fire-breathing monster of Greek mythology, with the head and breast of a lion, the body of a goat and the tail of a serpent.

COCKATRICE (see BASILISK)

DAGON The main deity of the Philistines and later of the Phoenicians, a monster, half fish, half man.

FAFNIR Guardian of the Nibelungen Hoard.

FENG-HUANG The Chinese phoenix, a male-female bird with the head and comb of a pheasant, and feathers of a peacock.

FIRE-BIRD (see PHOENIX)

GRIFFIN A ferocious monster, half lion, half eagle, which fed live humans to its young; symbol of eternal vigilance.

HARPIES Three hideous, winged monsters of Greek mythology, with heads and breasts of a woman, bodies of a bird and claws of a lion.

HERMAPHRODITUS In Greek mythology, the son of Hermes and Aphrodite, who, united in one body with the nymph Salmacis, was both male and female.

HO-OO The Japanese phoenix, ruler of the feathered race, which appeared only during the reign of a wise monarch.

KI-LIN A male-female form of the unicorn in Chinese mythology, symbolizing the reign of an upright monrach.

GARUDA A monster bird of Vedic mythology, and king of the feathered race.

GORGON (see CATOBLEPAS)

KI-RIN The Japanese Pegasus living in Paradise and visiting the earth only at the birth of a Sesin, or wise philosopher.

KRAKEN An enormous monster of Norwegian sea lore in the form of a gigantic octopus-crab.

LADON The dragon of Greek mythology that guarded the Golden Apples in the Garden of the Hesperides.

LAMIA or MORMOLICOE An iron-clad monster with a woman's head and breast, two cow's feet and two cat's claws, which feeds on the flesh of children.

LAMUSSA The human-headed, winged lion monster of Assyrian-Babylonian mythology.

LEVIATHAN A Biblical water monster, variously thought of as a whale or gigantic crocodile.

LINDWURM A winged monster serpent in Germanic-Nordic folk sagas, with scaly armor but lacking legs or claws.

LORELEI A semi-human watery creature of Rehenish folk saga.

LUNG A fire-breathing, scaled and horned dragon of Chinese mythology.

MAKARA A sea monster of Vedic mythology, representing the Spirit of the Sea.

MANTICORA A vampiric man-killing monster of ancient Tataric origin.

MELUSINE A European mermaid that married the nephew of Count of Portiere; her descendant Guy de Lusignan was King of Jerusalem and Cyprus in the 12th century.

MIDGARD The tail-biting or world serpent of Teutonic mythology.

MOLOCH A monstrous Biblical divinity of the ancient Ammonites to whom children were sacrificially burned.

MORMOLICOE (see LAMIA)

MURAKUMO-NO-TAURUGI The dragon sword of Japanese legend.

NEREID A sea god of antiquity.

NIDHOGGR The Nordic serpent-monster, representing the vulcanic powers of the earth.

NINGYO The mermaid of Japanese lore whose presence portends mishap or civil war.

NISROCH The eagle-headed god of Assyrian mythology.

OPHIUCHUS The Serpent-holder constellation, regarded by the ancient Greeks as the celestial reincarnation of Aesculapius, the healer.

OUROBOROS The serpent biting its own tail, an ancient symbol of eternity.

PEGASUS The white winged horse of ancient legend.

P'ENG-NIAO A semi-dragon bird of Chinese mythology.

PHOENIX In ancient mythologies, the Fire-Bird which rose from its own ashes; symbol of resurrection, good fortune and immortality.

PI-HSI A deity of the rivers in Chinese mythology, in the form of a dragon-tortoise monster.

QUETZLAL The plumed serpent bird, an Aztec symbol of the air.

ROC, or RUKH A gigantic bird of prey of Persian-Arabic legend.

RYU A Japanese dragon, one of the four sacred creatures of the Orient, able to live in the air, in water, and on land.

SCIAPODES A race of man in ancient India who lay on their backs, using their enormous raised feet to protect themselves from the sun.

SENMURV, *the Seed-Scatterer* A monster of Sassanian-Persian mythology, half mammal, half bird, symbolizing the union of earth, sea and sky.

SESHA The seven-headed naga-serpent of Hindu mythology.

SHEDU A human-headed, winged monster bull of Assyrian-Babylonian mythology.

SIMURGH The giant monster bird of Persian mythology, so old that he has seen the world thrice destroyed.

SIREN A sea nymph in Greco-Roman mythology, part woman, part bird, who by its singing lured sailors to their death on rocky shores.

SZ The Sword Ox, or Malayan unicorn.

UAZIT The mythological tutelary goddess of the ancient Egyptian North.

UNICORN A mythological horse-like beast having a long tapering horn growing from its forehead; symbol of strength and virginity.

SPHINX A composite monster of Egyptian mythology, including the human-headed Andro-Sphinx, the ram-headed Crio-Sphinx, and the hawk-headed Hieraco-Sphinx.

TATZLWURM A winged, fire-breathing dragon-like monster of Germanic folklore.

TENGU A fabulous winged creature of Japanese lore.

TIAMAT The serpent-monster of chaos in Assyrian-Babylonian religion.

TRITON A sea god in Greek mythology, half man, half fish, who was able to calm storms.

TS'UM'A'KS The sea monster of the Haida Indians.

VAMPIRE In Slavic occult lore, the reanimated corpse of a witch or sorcerer which leaves its grave to suck the blood of sleeping persons.

YU-LUNG A Chinese river monster, half fish, half dragon.

THUNDERBIRD A supernatural eagle in American Indian lore that created thunder by flapping its wings and lightning by blinking its eyes.

UNDINE A legendary female water sprite.

WEREWOLF A human transformed by black magic into a ferocious, carnivorous wolf-man.

INDEX

Page references in italics refer to illustrations